Good Grief:
The Journey to Life After Death for Families

Moriah A. Friend

Copyright © 2018 by Moriah A. Friend

All rights reserved. No part of this publication may be reproduced, stored in a retrieval system, or transmitted in any form or by any means, electronic, mechanical, photocopying, recording, scanning, or otherwise, except as permitted under Sections 107 or 108 of the 1976 United States Copyright Act, without the prior written permission of the publisher. Requests to the publisher for permission should be addressed to moriahafriend@yahoo.com.

Some names have been altered to protect the privacy of those involved. Conversations and details are best recollection of author.

Unless otherwise noted, scriptures are taken from the Holy Bible, the New King James Version®. Copyright © 1982 by Thomas Nelson. Used by permission. All rights reserved.

First Edition

ISBN 978-1718957367

To Jeffrey, Trinity, and Jasmine

I love you always.

—Mommy

Contents

Introduction 1

A Child's Grief 3
    Death by Suicide 4
    Expressions of Grief 25
    Why Did God Let It Happen? 55

Supporting Your Grieving Child 61
    Tackling Suicide 62
    Therapy 69
    Be Intentional! 76
    Free Memories 85
    Triggers 90
    Watch Your Mouth! 95

A Woman's Grief 101
    Layers of Dealing, Levels of Healing 102
    The Breakdown: Facing Me 108
    Take Care of YOU 127
    Moving on After Good Grief 145

Acknowledgments 153
About the Author 157

Introduction

Anytime someone close dies, life changes for those who are left living. Questions, doubts, and fear may arise, especially when that death was unexpected or sudden. This happens time and again for many people because death is a normal part of life. But what about when that death was not normal or from natural causes, but it was planned and on purpose? How does one deal with a loved one taking their own life? How does a child deal with losing a parent dying in this manner?

In 2015, these questions and thoughts became a part of my everyday life. Life had hit me and my family hard, so hard that many were unsure if or how we would recover. That was the year I looked death in the face, and that face was my husband's after he committed suicide. From that point on, everything changed for me and my children. I would soon find out everything I once knew and even loved would have to be tested, tried, and even lost.

I would need to begin rebuilding, from the ground up, my life and my heart. This rebuilding could only happen as I made the decision to walk through my grief process with honesty, transparency, dedication, and determination. This book seeks to provide wisdom and encouragement for individuals, particularly women and mothers, who may be grieving and/or struggling to find peace after the death—suicide or otherwise—of a spouse or loved one. In this book, I share my journey through grief as well as that of my children. Though their process will continue as they continue to grow and mature, they have, healthily and courageously, come a long way.

As you read this book, you will get a glimpse into what the grief process may look like for families. You will gain tips on how to walk alongside your children through it all. It is my prayer and desire that after reading this book, you will gain hope, strength, and peace in knowing there is life after death! This is my story and a piece of my testimony.

And they overcame him by the blood of the Lamb and by the word of their testimony.
Revelation 12:11

A Child's Grief

1

Death by Suicide

It was early in the morning on March 31. It was still dark out; the sun had not come up yet. As I rolled over in my bed, I noticed Jeff was awake and sitting up. (Because my son is named after his father, for clarity, I will use Jeffrey to refer to my son and Jeff to refer to his father). It must've been around 4:30 a.m., the time I got up to start my day. The look on his face was disturbed, frustrated, tired. "Are you okay?" I asked. "I just wanna get some sleep," he replied. As I thought about what he said, there was an urgency in me to pray for him at that moment. I was concerned. There was obviously something on his mind, something that was big enough to disrupt his sleep. I didn't know what was up, but I knew how much he loved his sleep. I went downstairs to the living room to pray. I prayed for him. I prayed for his mind. I prayed for myself and the children. I prayed regarding the day in general. I prayed in the Spirit a little. I just prayed.... In the darkness and stillness of that morning, I prayed. I was uncertain what to pray for or how to pray exactly concerning Jeff, but I knew I had to pray. When I was finished, I went back upstairs to prepare for the day. I tiptoed into the master bedroom and took my red uniform top out of the closet along with some comfy bottoms to fit over my now seven-month pregnant belly. Jeff lay in the bed and appeared to have been resting, so I quietly went into our bathroom to get dressed since it was dark in our room.

I don't remember if on my way out of the room we exchanged a "good-bye" or "see you later" or an "I love you." I can't say that is what happened, but I can say this ended up being our last moment together. Our last moment consisted of me looking over at him, the brief exchange of words in the bed, and then seeing him as I walked out of the room to head to work. Never in a million years did I think this would be the last moment.

The drive to work was a typical drive for me. My shift started at 6:00 a.m. and ended at 3:00 p.m. So, I left my home around 5:15ish to get to work a little early to open and set up the classroom where I was a pre-K teacher. There was the usual amount of traffic at this time of the morning. Base traffic came in shifts, the shift of folks who mustered or started work at 6:00 a.m. and then the shift of folks who were on their way home from working the night shift. I was on my way to work with this kind of traffic flow; thankfully, the drive was not bad at all. On a morning like this one, the drive was only about twenty to thirty minutes.

My day at the child development center on the Air Force side where I worked went just like any other day. I texted Jeff early that afternoon to check on him and to say "I love you," as I typically did, but got no response this time. I didn't pay it any mind though because I knew he was at work and likely just having a busy day. I ended up sending him another text asking him about picking up the kids from school. Jeffrey liked getting picked up from school right away, rather than staying for the after-school program while Trinity liked to stay at her school longer to play outside with her friends there. Jeff and I worked it out that he would pick up Jeffrey and I would get Trinity since they were at different locations. This plan worked when he was able to get off work early, which happened quite often. I often wondered and joked with him about what he did during the day because his hours were so flexible while mine were very strict.

Anyway, on this day, things did not go as planned. Because I did not hear back from him by 3:00 p.m. confirming whether or not he'd be picking up Jeffrey, I decided I would just pick him up. I picked up my daughter first and then headed over to my son's school. The drive from the Hickam side to the Pearl Harbor side that afternoon was anything but normal. The traffic was so bad getting from base to base. This was unusual because of the time of day, only 3:00 p.m. and the fact that on a normal day the drive was only about ten minutes if that.

The bases were all connected, hence the name Joint Base Pearl Harbor Hickam, making for an easy commute. On this day though, it was as if the base had shut down. The gates I would normally be able to drive through on base were closed, causing drivers to have to find alternative routes, which pretty much meant everyone was using the same route. The traffic was bumper to bumper, and it took me over an hour to get from the school where I worked to my son's school. Finally, I had both kids in the car, and we started off for our house. Driving through more traffic, we reached the bridge to Ford Island (a very small island within the island of Oahu). Driving across the bridge, my phone rang. The conversation went something like this…. "Hello, is this Moriah?" the caller asked. "This is she," I replied. "Have you seen or spoken to your husband?" the caller asked. "No, I haven't. Is everything okay?" I asked. "We have reason to believe your husband's AWOL. We sent guys over to your house earlier trying to find him," the caller says. "Okay, well I'm on the bridge now coming from work. Let me go and check," I responded. We hang up. I drove up to the security checkpoint on the bridge and handed my ID to the guard on duty. He let me pass.

As I drove the rest of the bridge onto the island, my heart was racing, and my thoughts were everywhere. I was completely clueless. What in the world? What is going on? What just happened? AWOL? Do people actually go AWOL in real life? I guess I was a bit naïve. I was used to the things I had seen in movies, but this was not a movie. This was happening in real life. Did that phone call just happen? What do I do? What will I find when I get home? I wasn't sure of the answer to any of the thoughts and questions I was having, but I didn't have time to answer them anyway because I had just arrived at my house. I knew I had to act immediately at this point. The caller alerted me, and this alert enabled me to use wisdom at this point. If nothing else, I was grateful for that phone call taking place at the exact moment in time that it did. Wisdom said to leave the kids in the car because what I would walk into was unclear. I quickly took off my seatbelt and told my eight-year-old son and five-year-old daughter to stay in the car. Being the curious children they are, they asked me why they had to stay in the car. I told them I needed to go see something and stated again that they were to stay in the car.

I unlocked the door to my house. I began calling out his name, "Jeff!" "Jeff!" No answer. The house was quiet. A little messy (though I hate to admit it), that's just the plain truth, but nothing seemed to be different or unusual at first glance. I walked through the living room, and as I passed by the kitchen, I noticed an open bottle of aspirin (he believed in taking one everyday) on the counter along with his badges and ID. Still nothing seemed out of the norm but I knew at that point that he was home. At this point, I figured he was just in the garage playing video games, and that would explain why he was not answering. I was wrong. I walked over to the garage door and opened it, but he was not there. I then walked upstairs. I got to the door of our bedroom and tried to open it but I couldn't because it was locked. I knocked and called his name, but no answer again.

Now, I was concerned so I quickly thought to grab my son's clothes hamper to use to unlock the door. Strange huh? Because his hamper was broken, there was a wire sticking out of it. That wire fit perfectly into the hole of our door handle, allowing us to pop the lock when needed. I unlocked the door and got into the bedroom, but still, I didn't see him. I noticed the door to the bathroom in our room was closed. I knocked. Nothing. I opened the door (because there was no lock on the bathroom door).

What I saw was horrific. In a matter of a few short moments I became engulfed in a thick and still cloud. There was no warning given to me about what I would be walking into. I was not asked permission about what my eyes would be forced to behold. What I saw was a rifle on the floor by the tub. What I saw was Jeff in the bathtub sitting up, dressed in full uniform except for his overcoat that he must have taken off once he got home. He was in his blue undershirt, blue camouflage fatigue pants, and black work boots, sitting in a pool of red blood. Tucked behind his back was a bulletproof vest. Next to him inside of the tub was a pistol. I saw a small hole in his forehead, on the left side, above his eyebrow, the white meat showing. I knew he was dead… There was no question in my mind.

My heart sank. Breath seemed to have left my body for a moment. As I came back to myself…I tried to process in the moment. I spoke aloud,

"Aww Jeff...What happened?" What happened? It was not tears that flowed, nor was it anger that built up right then. A strong sense of sorrow for him is what I felt. I just could not believe I was seeing what I was seeing. This just could not be real. This was just unthinkable for him to do.

At that moment, I felt such deep sadness for his soul. I immediately called 911 as I continued talking to myself and tried to think this through. The dispatcher answered, "911, what's your emergency?" she said. "I just found my husband dead in the bathtub. He shot himself," I replied frantically. She began talking more, asking me questions. I heard her call for an ambulance. "Jesus, Jesus, Jesus," I said at the same time. "Jeff...nooo! Jesus, Jesus!" Through all of this, my voice remained low, and I was surprisingly calm. I was calm but shocked and in disbelief. My mind could not even comprehend everything that was happening.

Still on the line with the dispatcher, she asked me how I knew he was dead. "He's dead. He shot himself in the head," I say matter-of-factly. To me, this was a crazy question but I knew she was just doing her job and needed to get as much information as possible. The dispatcher then asked me to check his pulse. Was she serious? Reluctantly, I reached across the tub and pressed my fingers carefully on his neck to check for his pulse the best way I knew how. Nothing—just cold. His temperature felt as though he had been there for a while, dead for a while. Wow… This was for real. The dispatcher kept me on the line, asking me questions. I articulated as best I could, all the while still trying to process. With my children…his children still in the car…I had to process this. I had to figure something out quickly. They were waiting. I had to get back outside to them before they came in the house looking for me!

As I began to walk out of my house from seeing the horrific sight of my husband sitting in the bathtub with a hole in his head from the bullet he shot through it, a million thoughts went through my mind. Time stood still and seemed to speed up at the same time. How do I tell my children? How should I present myself when they see me? Is it okay to be hysterical or do I keep my composure in front of them? I made the quick decision to call one of my neighbors, as I headed down the steps inside my house to make my way back outside to the car. I wanted to let her know what happened and to ask her to take the kids down to her house while I sorted everything out. I got no answer on the other end of the phone, but just as I stepped out of the house onto the front porch, there Anna was outside. I quickly explained and articulated as best I could. She agreed to keep her cool and give no details for the sake of the children. I opened the door of my Chevy Traverse to see the concerned looks on my children's faces. I let them know their dad had an accident but quickly followed up that statement with the news that they would be spending the night with their friends.

At this point, they must've known something was up because sleepovers away from home were something I rarely allowed my children to do. This day, the idea of a sleepover was the least of my concerns. Quickly, the concerned faces of my children changed to looks of sheer excitement. Not only were they getting to stay the night at a friend's house, but they were doing so on a school night. To top that off, I was letting them miss school the next day! As the excitement began to build for my two children, the horror, pain, uncertainty, and grave reality of things began to build inside of me.

As Anna walked my children down the sidewalk to her home, I turned back to my house, which no longer felt like my home. Within minutes, the ambulance arrived. I told them where they could find him, upstairs in the master bathroom. Paramedics marched in with their bags and a stretcher in hand. The neighbors began to gather outside. Whenever something happened in the neighborhood, the neighbors would gather. People liked to know what was going on and I didn't blame them for that. People were looking, and people were talking. This may have bothered me any other day under different circumstances, but today it didn't matter. I couldn't care less. The cat was out of the bag. The rug got pulled out from under me. I was naked, and yes, I was ashamed. But what could I do at this point? Nothing. The only thing I could do was live in the moment.

I was there. I stood there on that porch, leaning against the ledge breathing deeply and rapidly—in and out, in and out. I knew I had to be mindful. I breathed slowly, rhythmically, intentionally. I knew I had to keep calm. Now was not the time to completely lose it as much as I may have wanted to. Although life just left my family, life would be joining my family sooner than later. I had to keep breathing so that life stayed inside of me. The baby girl in my womb was still alive and kicking. I had to keep it together for her. I thought about her. I thought about how messed up her parents were: her father now dead and her mother wounded, broken, now single. It was just a mess, such a mess to bring an innocent child into this chaotic situation. But she continued to kick…she was still with me.

At this point, it didn't matter who saw or said what. I was in a complete whirlwind of emotions, yet at the same time, very calm. Perhaps I was in shock. I just believe God was with me as a father comforts, holds, and guards his children in the times they need Him most. My Father was there at that moment, keeping me calm, holding me, breathing into me as my breath tried to escape me. He sustained me right there in the bathroom and right there on that porch, and I love Him for that.

A couple of neighborhood kids stopped by, which was nothing out of the ordinary because our house was the "fun" house. Jeff was the cool dad. After school, many of the kids from the loop would gather in the back behind our house at the playground for football. When Jeff got home, he would join them. Many of these same children would come into our home to play video games and eat snacks or whatever food they could get their hands on. Today, however, that would all change. I quickly told the kids Mr. Jeff, as they called him, had an accident and they needed to head home to their parents. At that moment, I thought about their safety. I thought about the what-ifs. What if there had been children in our home when this happened? What if the bullet had gone through the walls and wounded a child? What will the parents say about all of this? As I stood there on the porch, with personnel going in and out, I tried to process.

I thought about the children, I thought about my children. I thought about probably everything I could possibly think of at that moment. The moment seemed unreal. This really happened. This was really happening. Life as I knew it had just shifted, ended, changed in an instant. I heard the paramedic say the "time of death" as they walked back out of my house. Although I already knew he was dead, somehow, this official statement seemed to almost take my breath away again. I looked away as they came out with his body now on the stretcher they carried. It was all just too much to take in. This was it… He was gone and was not coming back.

Now what? Now, I had to make some tough phone calls. I called my mother in Minnesota. I remember telling her with a somewhat quiet but trembling voice "Mom…Jeff is dead. He shot himself in the head." On the other end, I could feel her. She was shocked, unsure, worried, and unclear as she responded with, "What? Jeff who?" I knew she didn't understand me fully. She probably thought my son had had an accident with one of his dad's guns because it was no secret that Jeff had guns. After all, he worked with guns as a part of his job, but also enjoyed hunting and going to the range for fun. I quickly clarified. "Jeff Sr." She asked me if I had contacted his parents yet. I told her I had not and asked her to do so for me. She agreed to let his mom and dad know.

Next, I called my good friend, Reese, in Washington. Reese and I had been through so much together; our families had been stationed in Connecticut and Hawaii together since her husband was also in the Navy. They were stationed with us in Hawaii until a few months prior to the incident. Reese saw a lot in her lifetime; Reese could handle a lot, but I knew even this would be a lot for her. I gave her the news, her husband in the background listening. I can remember her immediately saying through tears a drawn-out "Noooooo...nooooo!" Her no's sounded strangely similar to my reaction in the bathroom when I found him. It was how she said it but also what was behind how she said it. I could feel the sadness, the heartbreak, the empathy toward him...much like what I was feeling for him. She had always made it a point to show love to him; that's the kind of person she was, loving. She told me she loved me; I responded the same way before getting off the line due to being unable to stop the tears from flowing.

At that moment, I had my first real release of tears, my first outward appearance of grief. It wasn't at the moment of seeing Jeff in the tub. It wasn't even in the moment of hearing the "time of death." It was in the moments of telling others who I knew loved him, loved me, loved us. It was in the moment of feeling the feelings of others. I'm not even sure if in that moment I began to grieve for myself. I was too consumed with the thought of his mother, his father, my mother, my children, and those who cared for him outside of myself.

With the first set of phone calls complete, I stood hunched over on my porch crying uncontrollably. The tears would not stop. This hurt so badly and I was helpless and alone. The worst thing that could happen had happened. I was literally on an island by myself. No family, no friends who I was really close with, no one who had been through the same thing to show me how to get through it…it was just me at this moment. I sat down in the chair beside me, leaned back and breathed. My stomach contracting and doing what it does in the third trimester of pregnancy, I breathed some more. Soon, the questions began again. A very nice man in a jacket with the letters NCIS sewn on came over to me and showed me his badge. He gave his condolences and explained what his job title was. He then began to question me.

As I pressed my finger onto the inkpad and rolled my finger across the paper for fingerprinting purposes, I could not even get upset. I just followed suit with what was asked of me. I had nothing to hide. I knew they had to rule me out as a suspect in his death. This was all too real…the kind of stuff you see on TV shows like NCIS. Except this was real life, my life. I was actually being questioned and fingerprinted at what was now a crime scene, which just so happened to be my home. Crazy. I watched as police officers wrapped the yellow tape around my entire home and my neighbor's home as well because we lived in townhomes. There was really no way to hide all of this! I knew this would be the start of a major investigation. I watched as a team from NCIS made their way through my front door, not saying a word to me. I knew they were strictly business. They had a crime scene to investigate. I watched them walk in with their scrub-like clothing on, covering them from head to toe. I felt for them. Although I'm sure this was not their first crime scene, nor would it be their last, I still wondered what their reactions would be walking into that bathroom.

The sun was starting to go down as I sat there on that porch taking everything in. The NCIS agent who fingerprinted me earlier came over to me and explained the Navy would be putting me and my children up in a hotel on base because I would not be staying at my house while they conducted the investigation. He asked me if there was anything I needed from inside the house. One of the female agents went in and got some of my personal necessities out of my bedroom. Everything else, I left there. I contacted Anna, letting her know where I'd be staying for the night and thanking her for keeping the children for me. She was so kind and thoughtful that she and a few of the other neighbors on our loop got together while all of the sitting and questioning was going on.

They gathered some clothes for me to hold me over until I had full access to what was in my house. Large shirts and stretchy pants and skirts were given to me in hopes, I'm sure, to fit over my large belly while keeping me comfortable at the same time. I was so grateful and will never forget that.

Now, it was time for me to leave and hopefully get some rest. I was tired. But sleep would not come easy for me on that night. A gentleman from Jeff's command was sent to the house to escort me over to the hotel. He offered to drive me, but I declined. I needed some time alone. I needed to just be by myself in my car where no one could see or hear me. I could be vulnerable; I could release a little more as

I drove. He ended up driving a government vehicle instead, allowing me to follow behind in my car. The drive from my house to the hotel was quiet, still, slow, long. Through teary and clouded eyes, I drove through the darkness. I cried and cried. I prayed and cried some more. This really happened. This was really happening.

At this point, all I wanted to do was leave the island and go home to Minnesota. Honestly, I felt like a big emotional baby, I just wanted my mom. I needed her presence. It was not going to be that easy though. Finally, I arrived at the Navy Lodge on the Hickam side of the base. I knew this would be my home until I was released to leave Oahu. The nice gentleman who had escorted me made sure I got checked in before he drove away. I walked into the suite… It was open and spacious with a living room, full kitchen, and two bedrooms. However, even with all of that space, I felt so closed in…like the world had closed in on me. It was just me now in that big room, no children, no husband, no military personnel, no police—just me. I sat alone in that room with just myself, my problems, my mess, my tears, my questions, my thoughts, and the innocent little child inside of my womb.

I remember sleep that night did not come easily, if at all. I was restless. I was afraid. Every time I shut my eyes to make an attempt at sleep, I would see him. I saw Jeff. I saw the white tub and the white walls of my bathroom. I saw the red blood. I saw his face, his head, and the hole that was there. I kept seeing this image, and so it was easier to stay awake and cry. That night my phone rang with calls and texts from friends and family who had just heard the news. Most calls, outside of my mother, I ignored. It was just too hard to talk about it. But I laid in the bed trying to at least rest my body for the sake of the precious life growing inside of me.

I knew it had been a rough and exhausting day physically but also spiritually. What I just saw and experienced, she experienced with me to some degree, and we both needed to just rest. I knew the next day would not be any easier than this day and so I laid there in the bed weeping and uttering what few words I could to God. There just really were not any words that could describe or express how I felt or even how I should've felt. I had never been in this place before nor had I ever imagined it.

For those who I did speak to on that night who asked me what I needed, my request was prayer. I knew I needed people praying for me. I was going to need a strength I would not be able to muster up by myself. I was weak and worn out, but I had to keep going because I had lives depending on mine. I was going to need my Father's love in a new way…in a way that He would soon help me to see and experience. I needed this love more than ever before in my life to fill me up and overtake me so that it would spill over onto my two, and soon to be three, children.

The day after his death, my two children arrived at my hotel room with a co-worker of mine, Tessa, who also happened to be a friend. She picked them up from Anna's house for me while I tried to rest and gather my thoughts from an eventful night before. As I asked them about their night away from me and they told me how much fun they had, I knew I had to do it. I had to tell them what happened to their father. It was just one day earlier that he had dropped them both off at school. That day ended with ambulances, medical personnel, and military police at our house. The only thing they knew that day was "Daddy had a very bad accident."

"Where's Daddy?" Jeffrey and Trinity asked excitedly. That was the first question my children asked as they walked into the hotel room to greet me after spending the night away. I quickly told them I needed to talk to them about their dad. Still unaware of what was going on, their hopeful and excited faces would soon change. "He's not here. He had a really bad accident with his gun." There was a very brief pause. "He's dead?!" Jeffrey yelled hysterically. "Yes," I replied. Jeffrey immediately ran out of the living room into the first bedroom. I quickly followed behind him to see him fall into the bed crying uncontrollably.

As I grabbed him and held him, no words seemed like they would be the right words. All I could do was hold him tight and say, "I'm sorry." As we sat there, his head in my chest still crying, I cried with him while silently asking God to help me and give me strength. Tessa, who was now also crying, sat in the bedroom now, holding Trinity as she sobbed uncontrollably as well. She cried in a way I had never heard her cry before. Loud sobs filled that hotel room. At that moment, I realized this was not about me. Yes, of course in many ways it was, but right then and there, it was about my children. It would continue to be about my children for as long as they needed it to be. I had to let them have their moment to break down. Going forward, I would need to let them have many more moments to break down. This night, the grieving process began.

2

Expressions of Grief

Death has a way of taking away a person's innocence. When a child experiences the death of someone close to them, especially a parent, the world changes. Things, people, places, and even God don't look the same. Nothing's the same. Life has just shifted in the worst way imaginable for that child. So how do they cope? They cope the best way they know how. Children grieve in different ways that are often unexpected, unexplainable, and even scary at times. Nevertheless, they must be allowed to grieve. A child's grief can make a parent or adult uncomfortable, but even still, they must grieve. It is through the grieving process that a child can become at peace with what has occurred. Immediately following their father's death, my children began to display their grief in a variety of ways.

Silence

I believe the saying "silence is golden" to be true, but sometimes it just isn't "golden" at all. Trying to break through the silence to get children to talk about their feelings or anything for that matter can be challenging in general. Trying to get a grieving child to discuss thoughts and feelings can be seemingly impossible, but it is something that must be acknowledged and worked through. Everyone deserves to have time alone and times of quiet. Whether you are an introvert or extrovert, there are just some times when silence is necessary. I found with my children, initially, my son was the more silent one.

Our conversations were often one-sided as I attempted to check in on him to make sure he was doing okay. He would respond with one-word answers, but that was about it. I could tell he really did not want to have those conversations but complied just enough to satisfy me. There were many times when I wanted more from him. I wanted him to pour out his feelings to me and to open up, but it just did not work that way. I had to recognize and understand his processing and grieving would look different from that of his sisters' and mine. In the early stages after his father's death, he never mentioned him. When Trinity mentioned him,

Jeffrey would just listen and stay silent. This was his way of processing and dealing. I had to respect his desire for silence while still understanding he likely had a ton of thoughts, feelings, and emotions going on inside of himself that needed to be tended to somehow.

Sometimes, children will be silent around their parents or those closest to them but will open up around others who they trust. Don't be offended by this. The very fact that they are willing to open up at all is something to find relief in. Although Jeffrey kept his thoughts and feelings pretty enclosed around me, I knew enough about him as my son to know there was more to what he was not saying.

Fear

Another natural reaction during the grieving process for children is fear. Children have many fears, that is no secret, but these fears can be intensified after the death of a loved one. New fears may also begin to surface. I'm pretty positive that it never occurred to my children to consider that they would one day be without their father. I'm sure, like most kids, they thought he was invincible and he would be around forever. He was their Superman. When this proved to be untrue, their way of thinking and living shifted. They no longer were in their comfort zone within their comfortable lives. No longer did they have two parents to lean and depend on. Now, they only had one. This, I believe, stirred up a fear within them that was not there before. This fear was the fear of losing me or the fear of me leaving them.

During the first couple of years after their father's death, this fear would try to show up. This fear sometimes may look like clinginess or separation anxiety, but this is when your discernment must kick in. There were many times when my children tried to stop me from going out with friends either by physically trying to hold me back by blocking doorways or by begging to come with me. I saw this fear the most in my son when I was preparing to take a two-week trip out of the country. He got teary-eyed, pouted, and pleaded with me to not go or to take him with me. Though this may sound somewhat normal, I knew it was deeper for him. He was afraid I might not make it back to him. He was afraid I would "leave" him like his father did.

Because I was able to recognize this fear was trying to rise up in my children, I was able to address it. I did not get upset with them for wanting me to stay with them or take them with me. I reassured them every time that I would be back or that I would not be gone long. I let them know that me having time for myself with friends or alone was important. When children have fears, it is important that we do not simply dismiss them. Take the time to listen to your children, not with your ears only, but with your heart so that you can discern what the real or root issue is. Remember, while their fears may seem insignificant to us as adults, they are very real and very significant to them.

Children who have lost a parent may suddenly feel very afraid because the covering or safety net that they once had is no longer there. They may feel vulnerable and lost, feelings that may cause them to feel afraid, especially if they've never felt them before. They may be afraid because they have been thrust into a whole new world, often without any warning or time to ease into the transition. This can be an uncomfortable and scary position to be in for any human being, let alone, a child. As parents and caregivers, we must do our best not to let these fears grow and cause unnecessary issues within our children while still acknowledging that they may exist. We can do this by addressing their fears, praying with and for them concerning their fears, and reminding them God has not given them a spirit of fear, but of power, love, and a sound mind (2 Timothy 1:7).

We can help to conquer these fears within our grieving children by being consistent and present in their lives as much as possible. This will help them to know they still have a safety net and someone who they can depend on and trust to be there with and for them. For grieving children who are afraid their surviving parent may die or leave them too, we can help them get over their fear by keeping our word and being responsible in our actions. If you tell your children you'll be back that night or in the morning, or by a certain time, come back! If for some reason you are unable to keep your word and something comes up, get the message to them that you are okay and will be back to them as soon as you can.

In the early stages of grief for children, it is not a good idea to go back on your word. This is a good rule of thumb for parenting in general; your word should mean something to your children. In the case of grieving children though, it is especially critical that they can trust what you say because they are in such a vulnerable state. Children pay attention to what is said to them, especially by a parent or someone they trust. A grieving child can be crushed when they feel like they cannot depend on that surviving parent to be there. This does not mean you cannot go out and have fun and have a life. Nor does it mean your children get to control what you do or don't do. What it does mean, however, is the little people you are responsible for need to be assured they've got you because they likely will feel like they've got nobody else in the whole world after the death of a parent.

This idea of keeping your word must be balanced by making sure your children know situations and circumstances arise that may cause you to need to go back on your word. Also, they should know sometimes you as the adult will simply change your mind, and that's okay too. The point here is to act as a reliable source of trust and safety for your children and I believe it starts with what you say *and* do.

Guilt

Whenever a loved one dies, it can be expected that children may feel some sense of guilt. This is especially the case when a parent dies. But what about when a parent chooses to die as in the case of suicide? How do you think children feel then? I believe the guilt that comes or tries to come is far greater than in "normal" death situations or death by natural causes. It is likely children will have the questions of why. Why did they die? They may wonder if it was something they did or did not do. They may wonder or even believe if they had been with the person, they could have kept them from dying. Thoughts of not being good enough in the eyes of the parent may run through the mind of a child. They may wonder if their behavior caused their parent to commit suicide. "Maybe if I listened more or got my homework correct they would still be alive." This guilt may even transfer over to the other parent if they are still living and present in the life of the child. This transference of guilt may turn into resentment toward the living parent. Children may blame that parent and believe the parent is at fault for what happened.

The scariest thing about experiencing guilt during the grief process is when the guilt causes a child to feel like they do not deserve to be alive. They may believe they should have died instead of their parent for whatever reason. Even beyond feelings of not deserving life, children may feel like they do not want to live anymore because they simply want to be with that parent who has died. This can be a tough situation to maneuver through because you must convince the child there is still a life worth living for them on Earth. This can be especially difficult if there is no belief in an afterlife. I believe it can be helpful for a child to know or at least be given the thought to consider that his or her parent is in a better place now (Heaven) where they are at peace.

This is a very real conversation I needed to have with my children regarding their father. I remind them as often as needed that he would want them to live and enjoy life to the fullest. I tell them he would want them to do well in school and as an adult to be successful. It may be necessary to encourage grieving children in this way, especially if they seem to be hopeless or have no zeal for anything in life.

On the other side of this is this idea of placing guilt *on* your children for having fun and for wanting to continue living. You may find your children seem to be moving on immediately after the death of a parent, or perhaps just at a faster rate than you. Though it may appear this way, it is not likely they have actually "moved on" in the sense of forgetting about the parent and not being affected by their death anymore. What you may be observing is your kid just being a kid! This is a good thing! What I love about children is their resiliency; they can bounce back from just about anything. They like to run, play, laugh, eat all day long, and pester their siblings. If you see this happening, and it occurs sooner than you expected, be okay with it.

Be careful that you do not make them feel bad for wanting to go play or be "normal" again after the death of a parent. For some children, this is their way of coping; for others it takes their mind off of the grief. Still, for others, it has to do with their age and developmental stage. Some children, especially young children, simply just will not comprehend what has just taken place in their life until later. Other children may fully understand everything but may just want to get back to being a kid again because death can be burdensome on a child. It's a weight they are not meant to carry. They may feel some relief of that heaviness when they are able to play and just be…much like putting down a heavy weight to take a breather and cool down.

While guilt is a very real feeling children may express or feel, it is not something they should keep as their own. It is important they know they are not responsible for the death of their parent or loved one. The only way they may ever know this is if you, as the surviving parent or caregiver, tell them. At the same time, you must be sure you are not feeling guilty yourself (see chapter 11 for more on guilt).

Curiosity

It is not unlikely for children to be curious about the circumstances surrounding the death of a loved one. While some would rather not know, others need certain information to help them process what has happened. Trinity was always the curious one during the period immediately following her father's passing. She was the one who would ask questions regarding his death. I attribute this to her being young, just five years old, when he passed. She still had a sense of innocence about her. I knew she probably would not be able to understand everything, but when she asked questions, I gave her answers. Adults must be careful here because although children may ask, that does not mean everything is for them to know.

I truly believe timing, discernment, and wisdom are important factors when talking to children about a death that has occurred. It is necessary to consider the child's age, maturity level, relationship to the deceased person, etc. Adults must consider the amount of information the child will be able to withstand. Sometimes, it is better to give just a little bit of information with very basic details initially after the death has occurred. Other times, more information early on may be more helpful for the child. The adult should ultimately consider whether the information they choose to share will do more harm than good for the child.

Having said all of this, honesty is still the best policy. It is never a good idea to lie to children. If a child asks, it just might mean they are ready for some level of discussion or information regarding the death. The adult must consider how much information is too much information. Questions to ask yourself if you are the adult being questioned by your child include: Am I ready to tell them what happened? Am I prepared for how they may react? Will I be able to tell them by myself or do I need support of my own?

I remember two specific occasions when my daughter displayed this curiosity. Keep in mind, both times I was caught off guard. The first time was when we were at my daughter's school about a week or so after Jeff's death. We had gone to say our goodbyes to everyone there, her teachers and friends, as well as the other staff we knew. I took her to the restroom and went in with her. It was a single-occupancy restroom, so it was just the two of us. As she sat there on the toilet, she was just as cheerful as can be chatting with me as she normally would. Then, out of what appeared to be nowhere to me, she began talking about how her dad needed a helmet for his head when he died.

This totally blew my mind. I had not yet told her anything about his "gun accident" involving his head. I had not quite figured out how to explain "suicide by gunshot to the head" to a five and eight-year-old. At this moment, I still wasn't ready. None of that mattered though because she showed me right then she was thinking about this thing and really was smarter and more tuned in than I gave her credit for. I say this because there was no other explanation for how she could have known his accident involved his head. The saving grace for me in this scenario was she did not actually ask me anything, but simply was sharing her thoughts.

The next time her curiosity sparked, I would not get off so easily. We were in the commissary getting a few groceries since we had not yet been able to leave the island. We had just celebrated Resurrection Day earlier that week. Trinity was and still is very artsy; in fact, she had the wall of my hotel bedroom where we stayed until released to leave the island decorated with art décor she had created. Through all that was going on, she still remained her spunky self. On this day in the commissary, she said to me, "Why didn't Daddy get up?" I asked her what she meant by that. She said, "Well, Jesus got up from the dead, so why didn't Daddy?" At this question, I was stunned as you can imagine, yet, intrigued and grateful at the same time. I was grateful she felt so free and open enough to even talk about this.

I was glad to see she was indeed processing and critically thinking about death on her own level. When she said this to me, she was not having a sad moment. We were simply walking through the store as we normally would. After I explained to her that her father's death was different from Jesus', she seemed okay with my response and went right back to hopping and skipping through the store as if nothing had just happened. I knew she did not fully understand death and how death works. I knew she would more than likely continue toying with the idea of her daddy coming back.

Tears

"Those who sow in tears shall reap in joy." --Psalms 126:5

There were a lot of tears shed after the passing of Jeff. The shedding of tears is perhaps one of the most common expressions of grief. I see the tears of children as it concerns death as a positive. Tears show they are not numb and unaware, but they are still able to feel. Don't be afraid, alarmed, or concerned when your children cry after someone has died because it is a sign they are dealing with it. Their body is assisting them by producing these tears. As a parent, of course, it does not feel good to see your child cry from deep hurt. But through my children's process, I've learned tears are a necessary component to them sorting out their emotions and healing.

I remember feeling some sense of relief or maybe a false sense of pride when, at their father's funeral, Jeffrey did not cry, so I thought. It turns out he did indeed cry. I just had not noticed it. My dad, who was sitting with us during the service, told me later that Jeffrey leaned over into his arms and cried. My reasoning for feeling good about him not crying was completely wrong.

Somehow, at that moment, I thought him not crying meant he was okay and unaffected by what was taking place. In actuality, I probably should have been more concerned if he did not shed any tears or show any emotions that day. I learned on that day this process of grief would be just that, a process. I learned there would not be any easy fixes for our situation or for the hurt and sorrow my children were experiencing. I understood I would have to let my children cry and express their feelings without the fear that they would not be all right eventually.

When my kids first found out about their father's death, the cries they released were like cries I had never heard from them before. It was such a sound that I knew only God could really understand at that time. It was like an inner groaning that manifested itself outwardly. It was a cry and a sound released from the depths of their souls. As their mother, hearing and seeing them like this broke my heart.

This initial cry was such a heavy and helpless cry. I would hear this cry again throughout their process but from someone whom I least expected it from, my son.

After his father's death, Jeffrey felt as though he now had to be the "man of the house." This was nothing that he said to me verbally, but I knew it because of his actions. I saw a complete switch take place in my son in the days immediately following his dad's passing. He began opening doors for me and insisting, and I do mean firmly insisting, I walk through them even when I told him he could go ahead. I can remember a specific instance when he held a door open for me, and I told him I had it so he could go through. I went back and forth with him a couple of times, but he stood his ground. He did not say anything but gave me a stern look and motioned with his hand for me to walk through the door. He did not flinch or move one inch until I gave in to his silent but firm command.

This was a bit comical to me, but I knew it was because of reasons he felt strongly about. This had to do with his loyalty to, and respect for, his father. I knew his dad had conversations with him about taking care of his sister and me whenever he was not around (underways, deployments, etc.). Jeffrey had apparently taken this to heart and went into complete "man mode" as much as he knew how. He began doing more than usual to help me. He began carrying and lifting heavy items for me as well as looking out for his sister even more. It was an unspoken thing, but it spoke volumes. It was as if he had taken off his little boy hat to wear his father's instead.

While I understand this notion of being the "man of the house", I do not agree with it. Children must be allowed to be children. Boys, in particular, must be allowed to remain boys and enjoy their childhood. Just because my husband had passed away did not give me the right to use my son as his stand-in or replacement. In my case, it would've been easy to let my son pick up the slack around the house and sleep in my bed with me to keep me from feeling alone, but that would not have been fair or appropriate. He was an eight-year-old boy, and it was my responsibility to treat him as such. As women, we must be careful that we don't place on our sons the expectations that we would place on our boyfriends or husbands.

I say all of this to say that throughout the grief process for boys, it is important they are given the permission to cry. The shedding of tears is not just for females, but for everyone. Often, boys are taught that it is not okay to cry or show emotion and this mindset, unfortunately, usually continues on into adulthood causing even more issues. It was outside of a library while we were still in Hawaii, that I literally had to give Jeffrey permission to be a child. As we stood outside of the library getting ready to head back to the Navy Lodge, I had Trinity get in the car first so I could talk to him. I noticed he had been very quiet, serious, and tense. He was carrying a burden that didn't belong to him, but he didn't know what to do with it. I knew he probably believed this was just his duty, to carry it, "it" being our family. I could tell he needed a good cry because he had been holding it in to be tough like a "man."

I had to release him. Looking him in the eye, I told him I appreciated him helping out. I told him I knew he was doing what his dad had told him to do. I told him it was not his job to take care of our family. I explained to him that he was not a man and I wanted and needed him to enjoy being a child, a boy. I explained to him how it was my responsibility to take care of our family now that his daddy was gone. I told him God would help me now that his father was gone. I explained to him what was not his job, but also what *was* his job. His job was to do well in school, be obedient and respectful, and to just have fun being a kid. By this point, his eyes were already tearing up, but he was still fighting it. I told him it was okay to cry and I did not want him to hold back his tears. I explained to him it was okay to feel however he was feeling. I remember grabbing him and holding him tightly, telling him, "It's okay." After repeating this and continuing to hug him, the tears began to flow. Not only did he let out a good cry, but also I could feel a weight lift off him as he sunk into my arms. There would be many more times when he would cry like this.

Children must be allowed to be children, and that includes crying when they are hurt, playing, doing age-appropriate chores, going to school, etc. They are indeed supposed to be trained so they are ready for adulthood and the world in general, but they should be trained on their level and according to the "way that they shall go" (Proverbs 22:6). This "way" is according to God's way for them. Often, this way is contrary to the way we would choose for them to go. His father's death did not negate the plan God had and has for my son. Yes, things would be different, maybe even a bit more difficult or challenging at some points, but my son still had to be given permission to live. His father's life had ended, but his had not.

It would have been unfair of me to put the burden of a man, the burden of a father, on his shoulders because it would have possibly altered the plan and "way" set out for him. Children must know it is okay and a good thing for them to live their lives even after the life of a loved one, especially a parent, has been lost.

Manipulation

Watch out for manipulation! Children can be very good at this, and many times may do it without even knowing what they are doing. I found that my son tended to fall into this category quite often. Dealing with manipulation can be tricky, especially when it happens during the grief process for children. It is important that it is seen for what it is and called out to prevent it from happening continually.

The times when I experienced this occurred when I was disciplining my son. He would begin to cry and tell me he missed his dad. Whenever this would happen, I would immediately know there was more to his story. He was crying and upset because I was disciplining him. He would tell me in that moment that he missed his dad (because we had different ways of disciplining). In other words, he was saying without actually saying it, "I miss my dad because I'm getting in trouble right now. If he were here, it would be different."

Although these words did not actually come out of his mouth, as his mother, I knew. It took me a couple of instances like that one to realize what was going on and how to deal with it. At first, when he would react this way, my heart would immediately begin to break for him. I would experience my own emotions of sorrow and anger all over again because of what my son was experiencing. I even had an instance where I began to cry after dropping my son off to school after having one of these conversations with him. For a moment, I felt so bad. Was I being too stern with him?

I wondered if I was being too hard or if the consequence I gave him was too much. But then it hit me, was he thinking about his dad before he got in trouble? Probably not. Does he miss his dad? Absolutely. What does missing his dad have to do with me disciplining him? I got it. I understood. It made perfect sense why he would react that way. However, I was not going for it anymore. The bottom line is that I am the one who is now the sole disciplinarian in our household. My style is indeed different from his father's, but that does not and will not change the fact that correction will still need to happen not just for my son but for all of my children whether they like it or not and whether they miss their father or not. I had to stop letting one thing get in the way of the other.

I explained this to my son. I let him know I understood he misses his dad. However, he would still be receiving discipline. Don't let grief get in the way of the needs of your children. Children need discipline, structure, and order. Here again is another time where wisdom and discernment are important because every case and every child may react differently. For my son, I knew why he would react so emotionally when he would get in trouble with me. So, I had to deal with it and let him know what he was doing and that it was and is not okay. We must not be so pulled into the grief process that we forget reality and even common sense. Children are going to be children, meaning, children (some children) are going to still try to get over on their parents in some way or another, especially if it means they might be able to bypass a consequence.

There will be times when your children really are having a moment of missing their loved one, but if this occurs during a moment of discipline, beware! Don't allow yourself to become emotional with your child to the point where the disciplinary action that should have occurred does not occur. Discipline, and then address the "I miss them" issue after. Or address it all at once, but by all means, *do* provide the necessary correction for your children. This is not a matter of being insensitive, but rather being a responsible parent in every season of life.

Anger

I recall a period where my middle daughter, Trinity, seemed to be going through a rough time. I decided to take her out to spend some one-on-one time with her. She had been asking to go to Yogurt Lab for quite some time, so that's where we went. We filled our cups of frozen yogurt up to the brim with candy and other goodies. We talked and goofed around, dancing in our seats as I tried to do some of the latest dances hoping for her approval of my execution. I never got the approval! As I made a comment to her, her response came with attitude.

Upon correcting her, the laughter and giggles that had just been there, turned to frowns, furrowed eyebrows, and tears. This was not just the normal reaction of a child who had just been chastised; this was deeper. I began questioning her about what was going on and why she was reacting in such a manner. I let her know this attitude and reaction was something I had been noticing for a while. I asked her to tell me what was going on. Did something happen? Is there something going on at school? Are kids mean to you there? The more questions I asked, and the longer I stayed on this subject, the more upset she became. She was definitely angry and bottled up inside. I knew there was more to it. She was angry and hurt but did not know how to express it. She looked like she wanted to burst right there in the restaurant as her face became more red and stuffy from all of the crying. Her body now tense and her voice now rising slightly because of the annoyance of my prying and prodding, I knew our fun outing together was over.

Now, we were both frustrated and upset. It was time to leave and head home. I left the subject alone as we drove home, but in my mind, I was replaying everything and trying to figure this thing out. What just happened? What is going on with her? Did I miss something? With her in the backseat resting quietly, I decided to let her be as we rode home in silence. As we pulled into our garage, I almost gave up on the topic, but I just could not do that. I had to get to the bottom of this. As she opened her door to get out, I told her to come sit in the passenger seat. I could tell she did not want to be bothered, probably thinking, "Here we go again."

I had to share with her my heart because I knew she probably did not really understand why I was being so persistent with my questions. I explained to her that as her mom, it is my job to ask questions. It is my responsibility to make sure she is okay. I reminded her it is because of my love for her that I need to have these kinds of conversations with her because I care. I explained to her when I see her in this state of being it concerns me. By now, she was calm, but still tense and looked as if she was holding onto something tightly that she so desperately wanted to let go of. That is when I asked her the million-dollar question. Until this point, I had asked her every question except this one: "Are you angry because of your dad?" At that very moment, it was as if something broke within her and her tears would not stop flowing. "Are you angry because he died?" She shook her head yes and cried even harder. I grabbed her and just held her tight at that moment and simply said, "I'm sorry."

Soon, the tears became sobs, intense sobs. She had not cried like this with me since early on after her dad's passing. As she cried, I spoke. "Do you miss your dad?" More sobbing and her body began to sink into the seat, her head hanging low. It was as if she was releasing bits of her pain with each breath she took in between her sobs. I told her I knew she missed him and it was okay. "He was your dad. You're supposed to miss him," I told her. "Never be afraid to talk to me about your dad. I'm not going to get upset if you want to talk about him," I said. I then began to ask her more questions now that she had just released some of that pressure inside. I knew she was more open now. "What would help you when you start to miss him? Would it help if we talked about him sometimes, like the good memories you have of him?" I asked. She responded with a yes. "Would it help you to draw a picture or write a letter to him sometimes?" Another yes. At this point, she had regained her composure, and her countenance had completely shifted for the better.

I needed her to know I was a safe place for her. I needed her to know her feelings mattered to me. I needed her to know how she felt was okay and normal. I needed her to know I shared in her pain, that as her mother, I could feel what she felt. She needed to know I had feelings and emotions just like her. I, too, still had some anger. I was angry she had to go through this. I was angry she was so angry. This was one of those moments I knew would come. However, it did not change the fact that it was still tough to get through.

As I began to share with her my observations and concerns regarding her behavior and attitude, the composure I had completely left me and I was now the one crying. Through tear-stained eyes, I told Trinity how much her dad loved her and he would have wanted her to enjoy life. "He would have wanted you to laugh and smile," I said. "Do you remember how he would always tickle you and do things to make you laugh?" I asked her. I told her he would want her to live life and not be sad or angry all of the time. "He would want you to be kind to your brother and little sister and for you to look out for them," I said. With her head and body now lifted upright, she looked at my now red and teary face with shock, concern, and intrigue in her eyes. I could tell she was taking my words to heart and found comfort in hearing about what her dad would have wanted.

We hugged each other as I sent her in the house. I stayed behind, seated in my car in the garage and continued to cry. I didn't want to do *this*. I didn't want to see her like *this*. *This* didn't feel good. *This* was the part that was hard, and I knew there would be more times like *this*. I was so overwhelmed at this point that I remember telling God I needed Him to help me. I was going to need some strength from on high to do this right. I was relieved she opened up to me about her father and felt like we made some progress that night but at the same time, I did not know how to continue this journey with her or my other two for that matter. This was one of the moments where it felt like too much…an icky feeling. It seemed like an impossible and unfair situation.

As parents, it is our responsibility to initiate tough conversations with our children. This applies to topics beyond that of death. These conversations will more than likely be uncomfortable for the child or you as the parent, maybe even both, but it still must happen. Sometimes, going through the grieving process with our children is going to require us to step outside of our own comfort zone to reach them on their level of comfort. Don't expect your children to be the ones to initiate conversations. It may be they very badly want to talk about their loved one who has passed away, but they just don't know how. It is possible they have some fears of doing so. Perhaps they think bringing up the subject will upset you or maybe a sibling. Perhaps they just do not have the words to express their feelings properly and so they hold everything in.

Parents should be that safe place for their children to run to whether in a physical sense or an emotional sense. It is important children truly know they will not get shut down for expressing themselves during the grief process and even just in general. I am constantly reminding my children they can talk to me about anything and ask me anything, no matter what. They are aware they may not always get the answer they want, but they know I will hear them out. It is important to note during times when children express anger due to grief, there should still be some guidelines set in place. Trinity was not allowed to just walk around and be mean to whomever she felt like being mean to. At those times, she would have to step away from the situation to regroup. She was reminded that she has a choice to be angry or not. I did not tolerate angry or pouty faces for long periods because, again, there's a choice in that. So, when moments would arise where I would see or notice some anger in her, we would take the time to discuss it. I explained to Trinity, that night in the car, anger is normal and is something everyone experiences.

Times of anger will come, just as times of sadness and joy will come. It is when anger seems to always be there that a concern should arise. During one period, I noticed she was always covering her mouth when something was funny. She was doing this because she did not want her laughter to come out. I remember asking her about this, and she said she did this because she did not want to laugh. So, even though her body was reacting, a part of her was stopping her from giving in to its natural reaction. She was choosing to be angry and heavy instead of light and joyful. I explained to her that while anger is a choice, she could also choose to smile, choose to laugh, and choose to have fun. Encourage your children to find reasons to smile and to rejoice. Even though their father was gone, life was still "good" for my kids.

From time to time, children may need to be reminded of what they *do* have when their focus seems to want to stay on what or *whom* they don't have. This can be done without making them feel as if their feelings don't matter. The point is to get them to realize they have been given a gift in this journey called life and this gift is meant to be lived out. Reassure your children they have every right to be happy and their loved one who has passed on would want them to be as well. I truly believe it takes more energy to be and stay angry than it does to laugh or be joyful.

Do your best as a parent to discourage your children from staying in a place of anger. Try to get them to articulate why they are angry at any given moment so they can recognize it and then more quickly come out of it. This may take time, effort, and practice but it is worth the energy. Children need to know they have control over their emotions and their reactions to people and situations.

3

Why Did God Let It Happen?

We hear it said all of the time, "As for me and my house we will serve the Lord" (see Joshua 24:15), but this was the real deal for me. I made it a point to never speak against or forget about God as I went through my grief, thus, encouraging my children to do the same.

When children are grieving over the loss of a parent, they are open and vulnerable to so much. As parents, we have the awesome opportunity and challenge of pouring into them, teaching them, and showing them God. It is not about forcing anything on them, but rather covering them (with no father present, the mother must cover) and being sensitive to their spiritual needs. Children who have lost their father need to know God sees, knows, and cares. They need to know He can and will father them. They need to know God is not at fault. This is especially true in the case of suicide, and I go into more detail later in this book.

After losing a parent to suicide, it is not unusual for children to blame or become angry with God. You may notice a shift in their feelings or attitude in regard to God. Where they were once open and excited about church and learning about God, a shift may occur there. Children may question why God "let" their parent die. They may hold animosity toward Him because of the belief that He could have stopped their parent from the suicide but didn't. It is completely normal for them to feel this way. In fact, many adults go through this during their own grieving process. If this does become an issue for your children, it is important that just as with every situation, you hear them out. Let them know you understand where they are coming from and their feelings matter. It is then important you give them the truth of the matter and that is that their parent had a choice.

We must always remember God gives us free will. While God is all-powerful, He still wants us to "choose" Him and His perfect will for our lives. It is not in His perfect will that we die prematurely. Along with God's perfect will, He also has a "permissive will." There are some situations and circumstances we choose to put ourselves into, contrary to His perfect will, but he allows or permits it. When this happens, I believe God still has the end goal in mind for us, but it just takes us a little longer and perhaps comes with more difficulty than He originally intended. Aside from the perfect and permissive will of God, I believe there are times when He gives us over to our own will. This would be the case in suicide. Death by suicide would not be in His perfect or permissive will because it would not get you to the "expected end" He speaks of in Jeremiah 29:11, "For I know the thoughts that I think toward you, says the Lord, thoughts of peace, and not of evil, to give you an expected end" (KJV).

While I have heard of many cases where people have tried to commit suicide unsuccessfully, many others were indeed successful. No one knows why God allows some people to leave the earth this way and others not to. At the end of the day though, it is important to reiterate to your children that the individual made a choice. Encourage your children to draw closer to God by building their own personal relationships with Him. Encourage them to express how they feel to God and ask Him the questions they may have. God is able to handle it and will not turn away from them when they come to Him.

Be real with them on this journey of grief. If there were times when you were upset with God, share that with them. This will let them know they are not alone and you have real and human feelings just like them. As you share, be sure to also tell them how you got over those feelings toward God because anger toward God is not a place where anyone should stay. Remind them God still has plans for their life just as He did for their deceased parent. Teach them how to see God as a God who feels just as they do. I truly believe God's heart breaks whenever one of His children goes astray in whatever way that may look.

God is grieved whenever someone dies prematurely and whenever someone feels like life is not worth living. Help them to get an understanding of what it means in the scripture where it says, "For we do not have a High Priest who cannot sympathize with our weaknesses, but was in all points tempted as we are, yet without sin. Let us, therefore, come boldly to the throne of grace, that we may obtain mercy and find grace to help in time of need" (Hebrews 4:15-16). They need to know God is a God who understands what they feel, and even how their parent may have felt in those moments before death. They need to know they can go to Him for themselves.

The grieving process is a great time to teach your children how to pray if they do not already know. While there are many sides and characteristics of God, children need, more than ever, to know about the God who is Love as they go through their process. They need to know He is waiting and wanting to hear from them and help them even through their sadness, questions, doubts, and fears. They need to know while He allowed their parent to make their own choice, He still loved them. They need to know He will not stop loving them because of how they may feel about Him or their situation. They need to know He stands at the door and knocks…waiting for an invitation from them…waiting to have a relationship with them (see Revelation 3:20).

While children may see God differently (either in a positive or negative light) after the death of a parent, it is my true belief that as the surviving parent, walking out a consistent life of serving God will benefit your children. Though you may not see it right away, your children are watching and listening…watching more than listening probably. Praise God openly as you grieve. Let your children see and hear you praying faithfully as you grieve. Let them see you with your hands lifted and tears streaming down your face. Let them see you on your toughest days still offering sacrifices of praise and thanksgiving. Teach them about why you do what you do in your relationship with God. They may fight you on this, but it does not matter because I guarantee you, they will remember this, and they will bless you and be blessed because of your example and your training.

Train up a child in the way he should go, and when he is old, he will not depart from it.
Proverbs 22:6

Supporting Your Grieving Child

4

Tackling Suicide

One of the toughest moments of this journey was the day I decided to tell my son the truth about his father's death. The truth was Daddy didn't just have any old accident. The truth was Daddy did not die of natural causes. The truth was Daddy took his own life. The truth was Daddy decided he did not want to be here anymore. The truth was I did not have all of "Daddy's truth," but I had to give my son what truth I did have. I battled with this for some months, believe it or not, before finally coming to a place where I felt ready and willing to address the "suicide issue."

Everyone knows suicide is not something that is really talked about. Sure, we know it happens, more often than it should, but it is still looked at as this taboo topic. So, I struggled with the idea of telling my children the truth. How could I possibly explain to them their daddy, whom they were so close with, made a choice to leave this world? As harsh as it sounds, that was and is the reality. From the moment I found him in that bathroom, not a day went by when I didn't think about how to explain this to my kids. I was consumed to a point with this thought. I feared how they might react knowing the truth. I was extremely concerned with whether they would blame themselves or want to take their own lives even.

Somehow, within myself, I reasoned them knowing would be worse than them not knowing. I figured, for the first few months after his death, I really didn't need to say anything more than what I had already said about him having an accident with his gun. After all, killing yourself is an act that should not and is not meant to happen, thus, making it an accident. I reasoned my initial explanation of his death was the best for everyone at that time and looking back, I don't know that I'd do it any differently. Although this was my decision initially, I was later encouraged, through much prayer and wise counsel, that being open with them would be the best thing for them.

The fact of the matter was I was allowing my children and myself to be robbed of freedom by the decision not to be forthcoming with the real, hard facts. I carried this burden, this load, and this weight of doubt, fear, uncertainty, confusion, and anger all surrounding this one piece of information. Though to outsiders it may have seemed like no big deal, just tell them what happened, to me--their mother and the woman who would now be solely responsible for them and their wellbeing--I thought this information could be a game-changer for them, and it terrified me. Suicide does not have to be a scary subject. It is not something that should be kept a secret or sugarcoated. It is what it is. The enemy tried to have me believe a lie. This lie was my children would crumble at the news of the suicide. On the contrary, though, the Word of God says "And you shall know the truth, and the truth shall make you free" (John 8:32).

As I mentioned before, there is still a way, time, and place to share information with children as it pertains to death. Although I had made up my mind to tell them, using wisdom was still just as important. I did not share with my children any of the specifics regarding what I saw when I found him because I did not deem it necessary, appropriate, or helpful for them, not to mention the images being a bit much for anyone to handle, let alone children. With my children being on two different levels developmentally and chronologically, I thought it would not have been wise for me to tell them about suicide at the same time and in the same way. I would need to be strategic and mindful of the language I used when explaining it to them.

When dealing with children of different ages, it is a good idea to talk to them individually so the content is fitting and appropriate for their particular level of comprehension. I knew my oldest daughter did not fully understand death, so explaining suicide to her was likely to be especially challenging. I set time aside to speak to my children separate from each other. I was very intentional with this time. I took on the task of telling my son very seriously because, to me, it was a big deal. I knew he would understand more than his sister, but also, I knew how close he was with his father, so I had to be sensitive to that in my approach. Honestly, it was a stressful time leading up to this day because I just was not sure how he would handle the news. Even so, I knew it was now something that needed to be done sooner than later.

As we sat at one of his favorite restaurants at the time, we ate and chatted about how his day went. I wanted to make sure he was comfortable and we were in a positive and pleasant environment. I asked him how he was doing since the death of his father. He kept his responses to a minimum. As our chatting back and forth subsided, and we sat in silence for a few moments, I knew it was time. I could tell he really didn't want to talk about his dad, but it had to be done. I began by asking him what he knew about his father's death. He explained his father had an accident with a gun. I asked him what he thought happened. He explained he believed his dad was cleaning one of his guns and had an accident that way. I then let him know that was not the way he died. I told him he was not cleaning his gun, but it was suicide. I asked him if he knew what suicide was. He said he did and I had him explain it to me.

I had mixed emotions once I found out that he knew what suicide was. I was shocked, surprised, and somewhat relieved. I really don't know why I was surprised considering how intelligent and aware he is in general. Yet, I was still a bit unsure, uneasy, and afraid. At this point, his disposition was serious, calm, and quiet. I continued…I explained to him his dad shot himself in the head with his gun. He did not even flinch. He simply sat there, as if he was unbothered, and nodded his head somewhat to acknowledge he heard and understood what I had just said. On the other hand, I immediately got choked up and began crying.

As I released those words from my mouth, I knew I could not take them back. The truth was out, and though relief soon came, it did not feel good in that moment. I was overcome with emotion; it was as if my heart began to break again as we sat in that booth in the restaurant. I was so sad and hurt for my son, displaying the emotions I thought he would have displayed, only he didn't. Instead, he reached out to me and grabbed my hand from across the table telling me it was okay. As I sat there crying, feeling weak, vulnerable, afraid, and sorrowful, he personified strength for me. My son was comforting me when I thought for sure it would be the other way around.

Those days and weeks before leading up to this day, I had been preparing myself for the worst, but his reaction was totally unexpected. Jeffrey was strong and courageous at that moment. This showed me he was going to be all right. Of course, there would be rough days, and other times when I would be the one comforting him but I knew he would get through it. He was able to handle more than I thought he could.

Often, we underestimate the power and capacity children have and we tear ourselves up on the inside trying to carry a load for them that we need not carry. Again, this is where discernment and wisdom have to kick in, but there comes a time when you just need to let the truth do what it needs to do, which is to make free. Truth must be released or be given the permission to exist for freedom to occur. If it stays locked up inside behind bars of fear, shame, guilt, etc., then freedom cannot manifest itself in the lives of those it is meant for. Give your children and yourself the permission to tell the truth and then receive freedom with open arms when it comes!

Although I had discussed how their father died, I had not talked about why he died that way. This brief discussion was had at a later date. I explained to my children just like people get sicknesses in their bodies, they can also get sick in their minds. When you are well in your mind, you are not going to harm yourself, but if you have a sickness in your mind, you may have bad feelings that cause you to do bad things to yourself. Just like we go to the doctor to get checkups or help when we are sick in our bodies, we need to do the same when our minds are sick. This was the way I explained it to them. I told them their father's suicide was not because he did not love them but because he may have been sick in his mind and didn't get the help he needed.

5

Therapy

Connecting both of my children with a therapist was and is one of the best things I could have done for them during their process. Within the first week after their dad passed, I had already made arrangements for them to meet with a therapist. I believe traumatic experiences such as suicide warrant immediate attention. It is important to check on children early on because they may not be able or willing to communicate what they are dealing with internally. Being unable or unwilling to do so can lead to further issues later on that could have possibly been avoided. Because of my own concerns, and the wisdom of family, I knew I needed to take them to see someone at least as a precautionary measure.

Initially, my children went to a "play therapy" session. This is usually more of a non-invasive setting where the therapist observes and engages in a conversation that is intentional, but still subtle in its approach, so much so that children do not feel like they are in a therapy session, but rather a fun, play session. My children went to the first session while we were still in Hawaii. The therapist did not engage in any conversation with them regarding their father. She simply sat in the room with them and observed them as they played with toys. She watched to see which toys they chose and what they did with the toys. She then asked questions regarding what they were doing, building, making, or playing. Interestingly enough to me, their responses and her observations of them through play revealed much about what they were experiencing and trying to process internally.

I know in our society therapy or counseling is looked at in a negative light, but it really should not be something frowned upon. It takes a wise and humble person to know when they need help and to actually get help. It takes a loving and mature parent to acknowledge and accept that their child may need more help than they can give on their own. We must stop viewing this type of help as being only for "crazy" people. There is no shame in seeing a therapist. As believers, we too must get to the point where we recognize in many cases and situations in our lives and the lives of those we know and love, therapy could be quite useful. It's okay! If we don't get the help we need…if we don't get the help that our children need, then we really *will* end up crazy!

So, let me encourage you to encourage yourself or those you know who have gone through traumatic experiences such as myself and my children, get help! Talk to a professional. You would be amazed by what sitting in a chair, or on a couch, for an hour in a quiet room while getting to just spill your guts to a stranger can do. As I mentioned before, all of the internal ickiness is not meant to stay there; it needs to be let out.

Once we got back on the mainland and got settled, I immediately began searching for a new therapist for my children. It was important to me that they see someone who was a believer and follower of Christ because this person would be speaking into their lives and would have some level of influence in their lives as someone they confide in. It was necessary our beliefs were the same for these reasons. I needed to know as they shared with their therapist, he or she would hear, see, and understand them from a God perspective. Also, because the nature of their sessions would be in regard to suicide, it was important to me the therapist would be sensitive to the explanation of it as it pertains to the afterlife, Heaven.

Seeing a therapist gives children a place to express themselves freely without fear of judgment or consequences because the therapist has no ties to them. It gives them the chance to cry and express raw anger behind closed doors in a safe place when they might otherwise not want anyone to see. I can truly say our therapist—she sees me as well as my children—was a God-sent. She is a spirit-filled woman of God. Her discernment is on point, and she is sensitive to the spirit of God concerning each of us. This means everything to me, to have someone like this who feels like an angel sent by God to listen, counsel, and encourage. I know she is not just counseling my children for the money or what she can get out of it. She truly cares and is invested in them. I know she seeks God before each session because she takes what she does just that seriously.

Jeffrey would not share with me everything he was feeling, but in therapy he was open. I found solace knowing he was releasing what he had been holding in, even if it was not with me. I just needed to know and needed him to know he had a place and opportunity to do so. If you are concerned about not knowing everything your child may share or express in a therapy session, don't worry. The therapist will share what needs to be shared when things come up that may be alarming or concerning. However, trust that once you find the right person, whether they share everything with you or not, your child will experience a sense of freedom and healing.

Many tears were shed by my children during their counseling sessions, tears that were not shed in front of me. I am always glad to hear this from our therapist because it means they are not numb to their feelings. It means they are experiencing moments of cleansing. Their outward expression of what they feel internally means they are headed in the right direction…toward healing.

Give a Little Extra

When parenting children who are grieving the loss of another parent or close loved one, patience is so necessary. Patience coupled with affection is needed in heaping amounts day in and day out. It is during the times that you least expect it when your child may reach out for a hug. Before rushing them off to tend to their chores, stop for a quick second and embrace them. There is a reason why they tugged on your shirt or called your name a million times in the last hour, and it was not to annoy you.

Consider this; they just want some love and attention. Perhaps they were missing their other parent or loved one, and your hugs are the only thing that makes them feel better. Sometimes, as parents, we have to slow down. Especially for us mothers, life can be overwhelming enough as it is when there is always something that has to be done. Make it a point to move a little slower. Choose your words and responses to your children wisely. Listen to their voices and the hidden pains and needs left unspoken each time they say, "Mommy, Mommy!" While you cannot, I repeat cannot, be Mom *and* Dad, you *can* give a little extra TLC when the need for it arises. A simple, gentle squeeze or kiss on the forehead can do wonders for a grieving child. It shows them they are still loved, still important, still thought of. Even in the midst of your own grief, the needs of your children must not be forgotten.

Remember they have gone through what you have gone through. Remember they are hurting just as you are hurting. Remember just as you desire to be loved and shown affection, so do they. Remember they may not be able to cope in the same way as you. Children need to be touched. They need to know someone cares. Extending patience and affection will help to keep the hearts of your children soft when it is so easy for them to become hardened. Say to them, "I love you" often. Remind them daily of your love for them. Let them know you're proud of them and they are good kids. Losing a loved one, especially a parent, to suicide can take a toll on a child's view of love. Remind them; show them love still exists. Let them see love by how you love them, treat them, speak and respond to them.

The grieving process is not the time to pull away from your children. Though it may seem to happen that way naturally, fight with all you have to draw closer to them. When everything in you wants to go and be alone, that's the time to go love on your children and to let them love on you in their own way. Let love be the glue that keeps your family together in the midst of the toughest of times.

6

Be Intentional!

Throughout the next few years following their father's death, I made it my business to be very intentional about letting my kids be kids. I believe that intentionality is extremely important when going through the grief process with children. It is important that grief is not allowed to take over their lives. I was determined, from the time we left the island and relocated to Minnesota, to make sure life was as normal as possible for them…as normal as normal could be under the circumstances. Because my children were very active, especially my son, I knew allowing them to still be that way was necessary. I enrolled them in a variety of extracurricular activities including soccer, basketball, gymnastics, and dance. I made sure they got to every practice and I was at every game and recital.

With a brand-new baby in tow, I was right there cheering them on and being that support they needed. On days when I felt like it was too much and a bit overwhelming, I made other arrangements to make sure they got where they needed to be. I knew life had to keep going for them. When it came to birthdays and holidays, I had to be intentional about starting and creating new traditions and memories with them. I knew it was my duty to assure they still knew they mattered. Even in the midst of death, life still goes on for children. For my children, while they were definitely impacted by the death, they still were very lively and always ready for some fun. I had to be intentional about creating an environment for them in which they could continue to live and thrive. I was intentional about connecting them with other children, new friends.

Moving to another place after the death of a parent can be traumatic for children, but you can lessen the blow by actively supporting them through the transition. One of the ways I did this was by finding and creating opportunities for them to connect with other children. If I saw the neighborhood kids out playing, I would encourage mine to go out and ask to join them. When they appeared to be apprehensive about stepping out to do that, I would go ask the kids myself. While they did not always like me doing this, they were always glad I did in the end. This helped get them back in the groove of socializing and having some fun with kids their age. Eventually, enough connections were made with other kids that my kids did not need me to step in to help them. Soon, the neighborhood kids began to flock to our new home to play in the same way they used to do in Hawaii. This, I'm sure, helped to establish a greater sense of "home" for my children.

Soon after having Jasmine, I felt so strongly I needed to be intentional about spending time with my older children. Whenever there is a new baby, the reality is siblings end up getting less attention in many cases, especially in a single-parent household. This is in no way an abnormal thing since new babies require more attention. However, when dealing with children who have just experienced a major loss such as that of a parent, the dynamic of this can feel a little more intense. I had to spend quality time with both Jeffrey and Trinity individually. It was at this time we began having our "outings." These outings were scheduled once a month for each child. When possible, I would mark them on the calendar for them to be able to see it, thus, building their excitement and anticipation and as a way to again keep me accountable to my word.

These outings became something my children looked forward to. We took turns picking what the outing would be. Sometimes, the outing would consist of a simple ride to the store with me while talking and getting a snack or treat of their choice. For other outings, we would go to their favorite restaurant for lunch or dinner. Other outings included going to play basketball or tossing a football with my son. While I dreaded doing both of these activities, because I am not skilled at either, I pushed past my lack of skills and did it anyway because the point of it all was to spend time together.

Please note the purpose of this intentional time is to focus on the children. It is not the time to be selfish and self-centered. Put the phone and other personal electronics and potential distractions away during this time and focus on giving your children "you." Beyond that, I knew it would be important and meaningful to Jeffrey. On some occasions, the "outing with mom" became an "outing with mom and the baby," but I would always ask them first if they minded her tagging along. While this may seem silly to ask them, I believe it was important to them. The purpose of our outings was and still is to give them alone time with me and only me. I say that to say there is nothing wrong with showing respect and consideration to your children. Even though my kids were always okay with their baby sister coming when needed, I believe it was the principle behind it they will one day hopefully appreciate. I believe they will look back and remember their mother was intentional about spending quality time and tried her best to make it work.

Family game and Bible study nights became another way for me to be intentional with my children during the grief process. This again gave them time with me but also created space and time for us all to be together. Once a week, the children got to lay across my bed as we shared and learned about God's Word together. During this time, they were able to ask questions, make comments, giggle, and just feel special because they were in my bed. This was a safe time for them, and I believe a time of bonding for us all. It was on these nights they saw God was still our God and nothing had changed in that area. This was definitely intentional on my part. Giving them a sense of normalcy, consistency, and family togetherness even in the midst of what looked and felt like family disruption. Everything around us screamed chaos and separation, but I was determined to keep us together. This was only possible because of intentionality.

Giving Explanations to Others

Talking about a deceased loved one among family is one thing, but what about doing so in the presence of those outside of the family? For children, this can be an uncomfortable situation, especially when that loved one was a parent. They may feel like they will be looked at differently, left out, or picked on. I knew there was a huge possibility the topic of fathers would come up at some point at school or during other activities with children, so I did my best to prepare my kids.

I asked them what they would do if someone asked them about their father. For instance, a friend may ask very simply, "Where is your dad?" or "Do you have a dad?" This subject could come up at random or during certain specific times such as the Father's Day season or sports activities. I wanted to make sure they knew what to say but also let them know not talking about it was okay too. Because my kids were new to their school, it was also very likely they would be asked where they came from and why they moved, thus, leading into possible questions about their father.

While all of these scenarios are innocent and pretty standard in the lives of children and school culture, I saw them as potentially serious and sensitive scenarios for my children. I never wanted my kids to be in an uncomfortable situation such as those mentioned and not know what to do or feel like they were stuck and alone. I believe supporting them by preparing them for ways to deal with those tough conversations helped them immensely and gave me peace of mind as well. On the occasions when my children found themselves needing to discuss their father early on, they handled it very well.

I recall two different occasions when my son had to explain his situation to friends. In one instance, when asked about his father, he simply told the child he did not want to talk about it. There was another time when he told a friend that he has a father, but he killed himself. When I found out he told his friend this, I was a bit taken aback but also proud at the same time. He seemed fine with his decision to give that explanation and unbothered by the fact that he told the truth about his dad. He still acknowledged his father, but also accepted the fact that the way he died was the way he died.

I can remember on one sunny afternoon when we were living in North Minneapolis; I was asked a question that tripped me up a little. "Do they have a dad?" This was the very bold question that was asked of me by one of the neighborhood kids who was playing at our house that day. She couldn't have been more than six or seven years old at the time. Jeffrey, Trinity, and I were on the porch when she asked me this. It caught me completely off guard and shocked me at the same time because of her age and simply the question itself because I had never been asked that. She had obviously been paying attention; kids are smart and perceptive like that. She lived across the street and was always outside so I know she could see who was coming in and out of our house. She never saw a man, and so she was, with every right to be, curious.

While this was such a bold and random question because of the timing and the way she asked it, I was glad she asked. It was the perfect opportunity for me to show my kids how to respond should this ever be asked of them in such a way. I simply told her, that yes, they do have a father, but he died. She seemed content with my answer and did not ask any more questions as she continued to play on our porch.

Children should not be forced or even expected to discuss a parent's death with friends, other children, or even adults against their will. When they are ready, they will share as much or as little as they want. In the meantime, though, they should be supported through encouragement, preparation, and compassion as it pertains to talking to others about the death they've experienced. Go through scenarios with your children. Make them aware of the way the world sometimes works, especially if they are school-age. Children can be cruel and ask questions for the wrong reasons, but they can also be very innocent and just curious about the differences of other children. Either way, by preparing your children for encounters with other children, and adults, they will at least be equipped with the tools to get through it unscathed.

7

Free Memories

Right after Jeff died, and we moved back home, it was all still so fresh for the kids, for everyone. They had just lost their dad and me my husband. Yet, how we viewed the situation was different even from the beginning. Because of this, I knew it would be important to keep them as connected to their father as possible, as much as they wanted. Honestly, at that point, at the beginning of the process, I could take it or leave it—that is the memory of him—because I was still angry and unsettled. But I had to be a big girl and offer my children opportunities to remember him and preserve their memories of him. I initiated this by printing photos for them to put into photo albums and materials to create a scrapbook about him.

Trinity was very excited about the idea of this little project while Jeffrey was more reserved about it. To this day, Trinity keeps photos of him in eyesight in her room, making different collages with the pictures every so often. Jeffrey, on the other hand, keeps his photos tucked away within his photo album along with a couple of memorable items of his father he keeps in a specific spot in his room. I have never seen him look at the pictures, although he may very well have in his own private time. My point in noting this is to show that though children may not choose to want to remember their deceased parent or loved one in the way that is expected or suggested to them, they will remember them somehow and in their own way.

Jeffrey's way of remembering his father was not through pictures but through sports, football to be specific. This was something they shared together. They would play football just about every day when possible outside of our home in Hawaii. When they weren't playing it physically, they were playing it on a video game. They watched football games on TV consistently, nonstop and too much if you ask me, but that's neither here nor there. Now that his dad has passed, Jeffrey has held on to that passion for football. Even though he has played many sports since the tragedy, his desire has always been and still is for football despite my efforts to persuade him otherwise. I say all of this to state that

I am not a fan of him playing football for many of the obvious reasons aside from the fact that I am just an overly concerned mother at times. However, despite my strong convictions about the sport, I choose to support his passion for it because I know it is a passion rooted deeply within his heart and it connects directly to his relationship with his father. In the meantime, I will just continue to pray for my sake and his. As mothers, we must allow our children to remember their fathers in the way they choose to remember.

Exceptions to the Rule

There may be some exceptions to the rule every now and then when it comes to letting children be free in how they choose to remember. When a father dies but leaves more of a painful mark in the lives of the family, especially his children, you may run into either one of two problems, sometimes even both. On the one hand, children may have memories of him that are so bad they choose to never speak of him or suppress the memories to protect their hearts. On the other hand, children may have very unpleasant memories of him, which may cause them to speak negatively about him whenever his name or memory is brought up. If this happens, it must be addressed.

While I am all for children having their own memories and choosing to carry out their memories in their own way, being disrespectful and dishonorable is never okay. This does not negate the truth, whatever the truth may be for what the child's relationship was like with their father, but it does mean certain parameters must be set in place. I believe it is extremely important that children are encouraged to honor their fathers while they are living and in the event of their death as well.

If a child who is grieving feels anger and animosity toward their father because of a sour relationship or the lack of a relationship at all, those feelings are definitely understandable and even warranted. However, it will do them no good to harbor those kinds of feelings nor will it benefit them to begin a pattern of speaking negatively against him in his absence. Should this occur, as the mother, you must hear your children out and then provide guidance about how to move forward in a way that can perhaps lead them to see something positive about their father and his memory.

This can be tricky to do if as the mother you also have negative feelings about him. Be sure you do not join in with any kind of slander or negative discussion of the father in the presence of your children. It is best, in cases like these, to lead by example. To be that example, it may mean more healing is needed for not just your children, but you as well. This is necessary so you are genuine when sharing with your children about the memory of their father and why honor is important. Even though addressing these tough issues and feelings with your children is critical to them healing properly, so is allowing them to speak how they feel. Please do not misunderstand; children will remember in their own way as stated before, but the way in which they carry out those memories is what should be addressed if need be. There is a way to express negative feelings and emotions about their father without bashing or slandering his name, and this applies to mothers as well.

"Honor your father and mother," which is the first commandment with promise: "that it may be well with you and you may live long on the earth."
Ephesians 6:2-3

8

Triggers

Along this journey, there will more than likely be events that take place or words spoken that act as triggers for your children. It is important you are aware and on the lookout for known triggers as well as potential ones. A trigger can be anything that reminds a child of a traumatic event they've experienced such as the death of a parent. These triggers usually cause a negative reaction, thought, or emotion in the child because it takes them back to a place—a scary, uncomfortable, or sad place—where they don't want to be mentally. In other words, these kinds of triggers force the child to remember what or even who they may not necessarily want to remember at that time.

While it is impossible to shield children from everything, there may be some situations or events that you may want to exclude them from to protect them emotionally, especially in the early stages of grief. Funerals for others (e.g., friends and family members), may not be the best environment for a child who has just lost their parent. Attending someone else's funeral may only evoke the same emotions they had when their parent died or when they were at their funeral.

While on the topic of funerals, let's discuss them further. When a parent dies, there may be some hesitation as to whether the child should attend the home-going service because of their age or for fear of them not being able to handle it. This came up as an issue with my own children. When their father died, he was given two services. One service was a memorial service held in Hawaii before we moved that was put on by the Navy. This service was to honor him as someone who served his country and gave those who were a part of the Uniformed Services family an opportunity to pay their respects. His second service was the home-going service we put on for him in his hometown of Minnesota.

After seeing how emotional my children were at his memorial service, I had family advise me to consider not having them attend his funeral in MN. I gave it some careful thought but decided it would be best for them to be in attendance. I felt like it would be a good time for them to have further closure about his death. They got to be a part of the burial ceremony held at Fort Snelling National Cemetery, where his body was laid to rest, and they received official pins, other special items, and a flag for his service in the military. Aside from all of this, choosing to have them attend both services put them in a position to be loved on by family and friends who cared about them. As people spoke and honored him, my children were able to hear stories about their father from the perspective of others who had relationships with him. They got to get a glimpse of so many people whose lives were touched by their father. I believe it is important to provide children with opportunities to gain closure in situations such as death.

Now let's get back to triggers. Other triggers can include holidays such as Thanksgiving and Christmas or Father's and Mother's Day. Holidays are normally a time when families are together creating memories, so this can be tough for children who have just experienced a break in their family. Whenever Father's Day season comes around, I am always mindful of how my children may feel. I make sure to have a conversation with them before the actual day or before heading into a situation where I know the topic will come up. I check in with them to see how they are doing and feeling and ask them if they are going to be okay.

So far, there have been no incidents where they were unable to handle themselves on that day, but I still do this as a precautionary measure to help to ensure they are comfortable and prepared. Though there are unfortunately many children without fathers, because mine once had theirs and suddenly were without him, these check-ins are still important around this time of the year. If ever your children feel triggered, by situations like these, it is best to be understanding and compassionate rather than annoyed.

Other triggers may include going to familiar places or being around people who remind them of their loved one. Keep in mind, at some point children will have to get used to their new life and adjust to their environment, even when potential triggers are there. However, early on, when the traumatic experience is still fresh, as parents and caregivers, we must use wisdom and act as a protector for them when needed to avoid any further or unnecessary trauma.

Some triggers may totally catch you off guard in that they are not packaged in the way you expect. The smallest or most unusual things may set your children off. But it's important that you be sensitive to their needs even during those times. I remember this happening for us one day out of the blue. I heard a loud bang and ran to the front door to see what happened. Jeffrey, Trinity, and a friend were outside on the porch playing when they witnessed a car accident. They were all pretty shaken up, especially Trinity, who was shaking and crying as she grabbed me, holding on to me tightly. That accident had triggered something in her, reminding her of how her dad had an "accident" and died. She was afraid someone in the crash died as well. Thankfully, they were okay.

While the car accident was totally unrelated to her father's death, in my opinion, I still had to take time at that moment to comfort her. I explained to her everything was going to be all right with the individuals in that crash and she didn't have to be afraid. She was able to regroup and continue playing soon after that. Every child's triggers may be different, and you may even have triggers of your own. Just make sure to pay attention, be aware, and not become paralyzed by them. Children must learn how to function in a world full of triggers and potential triggers. They can do this with your help and support.

9

Watch Your Mouth!

Feelings that may not be announced right away or openly by grieving children include rejection, abandonment, shame, and worthlessness. However, they will probably show up at some point. These feelings often show up in subtle ways commonly through words spoken by children. These words can be spoken in the form of a vow. What children say and how they say it reveals much about how they truly feel about themselves although they may not realize it. They may actually try to hide their true feelings about themselves, but their words will often tell on them. Matthew 12:34 tells us, "...out of the abundance of the heart the mouth speaks." Proverbs 4:23 tells us out of the heart flows the issues of life.

This lets us know whatever is going on on the inside, whether it be sorrow, fear, rejection or insecurity, anger, or anything else connected to grief, it will show itself by what is spoken. It is for this reason, as guardians over our children, we must make sure they know who they are and that they are constantly being given truths to hold onto. During times when they want to impulsively say something that is contrary to the truth, their hearts will remind them and cause them to pause, rethink, and collect themselves. Doing this will help to ensure what comes out of their mouth, even during times of grief, is truth. This truth promotes health, wholeness, and positivity.

Because of the immature state of a child, it is likely words will be spoken more freely and carelessly. Children have a tendency to be very honest and uncut with what they say. In other words, children, especially young children, do not have a filter that activates when they speak. They simply say how they feel and express their opinions at any given moment and, however it comes out, it just comes out! This innocence and freedom children have can definitely be used in a positive way, but as we know, to every positive, there is bound to be a negative. It is for this reason we must pay close attention to what comes out of our children's mouths as much as possible in a general sense, but especially during the process of grief.

When children grieve, their emotions may be out of whack as well as the way they view themselves and the world around them. This may cause them to say things they may not even mean, or they may say things they do actually mean or feel on the inside about themselves and others. Either way, idle words can be dangerous, innocently spoken or not. It is unrealistic to think we will know everything they are thinking and saying, but what we do know is what we are accountable for. For the moments when they are out of our presence, hopefully, whatever we have taught them will kick in.

Be watchful of the child who is always saying "I can't do this" or I'll never do that." A child who has a difficult time in school may say things like "I'm never going to be able to do this!" or "I'm not good at anything!" While these may seem like innocent phrases it still stands that there is power in words. Whether these words are out of the mouths of immature children or mature adults doesn't matter. Teach your children about the power they have in their mouths. Teach them about the power they were given to be able to choose how they use their mouths. Talk to them about what it means to bless and curse and to speak life or death. They need to be aware of the power they hold and how to use it in a way that is pleasing to God and beneficial to their lives.

I am constantly reminding my children to be mindful of what they are saying. My middle daughter is an artist who tends to be very critical of her work and often gets discouraged. At these times, she may speak negatively about herself or her work. When I hear her, I quickly correct her by giving her something positive to say about herself and her work, reminding her of the power of her tongue.

If you have children who sometimes or oftentimes speak negatively about themselves, others, or life in general, it may be time to change things up a bit. Children are going to have their moments where their words and expressions are not positive or ideal; that's normal. However, when it happens regularly or excessively, that's when your concern should heighten. Be sure to listen and hear them out. Ask questions and take those moments to be open with your child. Provide encouragement and words of affirmation to them.

For my children, I wrote affirmations and confessions for them to read aloud every day because I knew with the death of their father came the potential for blows to their self-esteem, self-worth, and faith. What is spoken at a young age can have a direct effect on what happens at an older age in a person's life. The bottom line is that words are seeds and seeds grow.

Even during times of grief, we must be careful not to allow the wrong things to come out of our mouths or the mouths of our children. It can be easy to just say whatever comes to mind, especially during times when we or our children are hurting, angry, afraid, and unsure of what life may bring. It is during those times we must be ever so careful of what we speak or allow to be spoken. Whether we or our children mean it or not, those words will have to take form, if not now, then later on in the future. It is wise to teach children the art, the lost art if you ask me, of thinking before speaking. This concept is often thrown around, but seldom put into practice it seems.

Let's think for a moment, how much different would our lives be if we had slowed down and taken a moment to think before speaking? What about your parents? What if they hadn't called you stupid? What if they had never told you that you'd be nothing or you were nothing special? Would your life be different? Would you have made different decisions? Would you have surrounded yourself with different people? What if they had thought before they spoke negatively about you? Perhaps they would have realized they were doing so because of their own hurt, pain, anger, or grief. As adults, many of our major decisions and life outcomes have already taken place. We may even be at a place of reaping, either negatively or positively, based on what was spoken over us or from our own mouths.

While it may seem like what's done is done, there is still hope for us and especially our children. They have more growing, living, and decision-making to do. The grieving process is the perfect time to encourage and help them to be mindful of the world they have the ability to create for themselves simply by choosing their words carefully.

Death and life are in the power of the tongue,
And those who love it will eat its fruit.
Proverbs 18:21

A Woman's Grief

10

Layers of Dealing, Levels of Healing

There are levels and layers that a person must go through during the process of grief and healing. It is not something that just happens overnight. Yes, with God all things are possible, but even in that, there is still a process to walk out. My healing did not happen right away. As a matter of fact, I found myself at times frustrated because I wanted to be fully healed sooner than I was. Never let anyone tell you to just "Get over it" or even the common phrase people say as encouragement, "Stay strong." I would like to suggest the complete opposite is needed as advice when it comes to grieving and healing. Take the time it takes for you to deal. Every person is different, and every situation is different.

While I believe there is a point when you must come out of your grief, I do not believe that point in time is the same for everyone. When you are grieving, that is not the time to try to stay strong. It is during that time you will probably be at your weakest point. Be okay with that. Sit in that. It is when we are weak that God's strength can take over for us. "And He said to me, 'My grace is sufficient for you, for My strength is made perfect in weakness.' Therefore, most gladly I will rather boast in my infirmities, that the power of Christ may rest upon me" (2 Corinthians 12:9). The grieving process is not the time to be full of pride. Rather, it is the perfect time to humble yourself in whatever way that might mean for you as an individual. For me, it meant asking for help.

By the age of nineteen, I was already married, a mother, and had moved out of state with my new family. Because of this, I was used to doing things on my own. I had to do things on my own because I had my own family. When Jeff died, all of that changed. It was no longer he and I against the world; it was just my now three children and me. I was not used to being a single mother. Although being a military wife gave me a taste of what single life was at times, it was not quite the same. Humility taught me I could not do everything on my own. Humility taught me I did not have to do everything on my own because there were people who were willing and wanting to help me. Humility taught me moving back home to live with my mother would be a wise decision.

This was not necessarily the easiest decision because, again, I was so used to being on my own. Pride told me I did not need anyone. Pride laughed at me for having to go back home to my mom. Pride pointed the finger at me because I was now the single mother I never wanted to be. But humility told me it was all right. I learned to take and accept the help I needed. I began to ask my mom to watch the kids for me so I could take some time out for myself. To some, this seems like a normal request, but for me, it was not. Asking for help and taking help even when it seemed forced upon me by those who loved me, was a big step for me. Had I stayed in the mindset of "I got this" and "I don't need nobody," I would not have walked into my healing as quickly as I did. The truth is that I *did* need somebody. The truth is that I did not have it all together or figured out. The truth is I could not have gone through my process alone.

The fact of the matter is I was at a low point after Jeff's death. So many questions and thoughts consumed my mind all at once, yet I couldn't really seem to process them right away. Life still had to go on. I moved back to Minnesota with my two oldest children, the youngest still in my belly. Just two short months after that, I gave birth to my youngest daughter. Although I was overjoyed and amazed at this new life God had allowed to come into the earth, I still found myself troubled, sad, unsure, and afraid.

There were many days when I just wanted to scream. In fact, there were many days when I did scream, and my oldest children can attest to that. I am not ashamed to say on days when I felt overwhelmed, I screamed. I literally stopped whatever I was doing and screamed at the top of my lungs—usually in the house or car while driving. As you can imagine, this came as a shock to my children when I did this. I would do this because I had to let out what I was feeling on the inside in some way.

Sometimes, when you are grieving, your emotions and thoughts will be all jumbled, and you may feel out of sorts. You may feel tense, heavy, and off-kilter. When this happens, scream! I mean really just let it out. I suggest doing this behind closed doors, but by all means, do it! You may look and sound crazy but trust me, you will feel better after. All of that stuff (pain, stress, etc.) is not meant to stay inside you. Sometimes, words just won't suffice. Sometimes, you will not even have the words to express what you are feeling. The act of screaming can do the trick. It can help to release some of the pressure and anguish you may be experiencing. If you have children, explain to them why you are screaming so they are not alarmed or afraid. I let my children know my screaming was not about them and I was okay but just needed to let out a good scream. Feel free to invite your children to scream with you. It can be a good way for the whole family to relieve some tension. This can also help to open a stiff atmosphere because of the heaviness grief can bring.

I believe just as the walls of Jericho came down in Joshua 6:20 after the children of Israel shouted, so too can the walls of grief come down. After shouting/screaming, it's almost like a shattering that takes place as in a shattering of glass, ice, or a ceiling. With my children, we would see who could scream the loudest. On other days, instead of screaming, we would purposely laugh aloud as a way of release and relief. Screaming is my favorite way of releasing what needs to be let out, but this can also work with belching. On a couple of occasions, we would see who could belch the loudest. This didn't bring much relief to me, but it was definitely a favorite for my children and a great way to shift the atmosphere around us.

Whatever method you use, just make sure it is safe and not at the expense of someone else like your children or those closest to you. Never is it okay to hurt someone else to make yourself feel better. Even in the grieving process, as adults, we are still responsible for our actions and reactions. If ever there is a time where you feel unable to stand in your responsibilities, please reach out and get help and don't feel bad about doing so.

11

The Breakdown: Facing Me

What I love about God is He is everything I need Him to be. There is such a depth to Him and His love that is really incomprehensible, yet that is who He is. I learned so much about the "I am" of God during my process. Soon after I moved back to Minnesota and gave birth to Jasmine, God began to really deal with me about Jeff's death. His funeral had already come and gone, the baby was born, and the kids were back in school, so it was time to refocus and deal so I could *really* begin to heal. Until this point, I had not really done much to foster healing for myself because things had moved so quickly and I had three young children who needed my attention. But as things slowed down, I knew it was time, my time to break down and be broken down.

I had to face the music, and that meant I had to face me. Before I could face me though, I had to face Jeff and release him. I wrote a letter to him sharing all of the thoughts, feelings, and anger I felt surrounding his death. I expressed, as best I could on paper, the pain and sorrow I was feeling. I read it aloud because though he was not there to read it or hear it, it still needed to be let out. After reading the letter through blurred, teary eyes, I made the decision to burn it.

This was symbolic for me. I needed to release what I had been holding against him. There was no need for me to save the letter, the hurt, the anger, the pain, etc. I needed to release it once and for all because the reality was he was not coming back so none of it mattered anymore. All of the "shoulda, coulda, wouldas" were no longer a factor. It was through this seemingly simple, yet extremely difficult exercise I began to face my true feelings and start the process of forgiveness. Notice I said my forgiveness toward Jeff was a process. It was a process that first started with a decision. The process became easier once I released him and became open to seeing him through the eyes and heart of God. It was God who gave me compassion for him so I could not stay in a place of anger very long.

I began to realize only someone who was already hurting would hurt themselves and others. I no longer saw Jeff's suicide as something he did to intentionally hurt our children or me. But I now saw him as a man who was hurting, crying out for help, and doing the best he thought he could do for himself and his family at that time. I now viewed him from the perspective of a soul and not the husband who tore our family apart. Now, I could hope and pray in his final moments on this earth, he had a chance... a split second even, to speak to God and get things right and be restored.

It is true what they say--Forgiveness is not for the other person; it is for you! This wasn't about him anymore; it was about me. We must be mindful of this when going through a process of grief. That loved one is gone now, but you are still here, needing to live and deal with reality. You cannot do this effectively if you are too busy holding on to that person and the past that involved what they did or did not do. Your deceased loved one will move on into the afterlife with or without your blessing, but it's up to you to decide whether or not you will move on into your present and future life. Make the choice to forgive!

Forgiveness will change your vision and perspective on things because you no longer look at people or situations with your natural eyes, but with God's. Forgiveness has the ability to change you so much so that the only person you now see is yourself as the one in need of forgiveness and change. Me making the decision to forgive and release Jeff freed me but also forced me to see myself. What I saw was not a pretty picture.

On the outside, I may have appeared to be polished and put together, but inside I was cracked, shattered even, and ugly. There were many times during my process I had to say to my own self, "What is wrong with you? Get it together!" Often, as married women, we tend to lose ourselves. This can be especially true if you marry and have children at a young age. I had become so wrapped up in Jeff and my children and my duties as a wife and mother, I didn't know who I was. His death forced me into a position of having to see myself for who I was, and I didn't like what I saw. It was necessary that I see myself in this state so I could fully heal. Now, we two were no longer one, and I had no excuse, no reason why I could not see me. My prayer became "God show me myself." He did just that. What I saw were pride and shame. What I saw was a mask over my face.

I remember one Sunday morning as I stood in the congregation at my then new church home as praise and worship was taking place. I heard the Lord clearly tell me to take off my wedding ring. At this point, Jeff had been dead for probably only close to two months. So, you might say, well what was the big deal? Why should I have to stop wearing my ring so soon after his death? Well, for me it was a big deal. I knew exactly why I had to take it off. As the Holy Spirit spoke those words to me, I literally bawled my eyes out as I removed the ring from my finger right there during service. I knew it was something I needed to do at that exact moment in time and so I didn't question God. Still, though, it was a very tough thing for me to do but for all the wrong reasons. I was so tied to the image of marriage.

I was always big on wearing my ring because, to me, it made a statement beyond the obvious. It made me feel good about myself. I never wanted to be a single mother. I never wanted to be the woman with a bunch of children and no father. But God has a way of humbling us when we become puffed up. This act of removing my wedding band humbled me. Now, I was that woman with a bunch of kids and no father anywhere in sight. I wondered what people would think of me. When they saw me with my two kids, pregnant belly, and no ring would they make assumptions? I had to be brought low; I had to be stripped of my "happily ever after" image.

Jeff's death alone was probably the ultimate humbling factor in that there was no "happily ever after" ending. It was more like an abrupt and unexpected announcement to the entire world that everything was not neat and perfect in our lives. This is where I saw the shame when I saw myself. I was ashamed of the way things happened. I was ashamed of the fact that my marriage didn't last. This is not to say his life ended the way it did because of our marriage, but rather our marriage ended because of his suicide. As a spouse, of course, you want to be able to hold your marriage together. But that just did not happen in our case. I was ashamed of the fact that I couldn't help him. I was ashamed I didn't even know he needed to be helped in that way.

I felt shame when I thought about my children being fatherless. There were so many issues within myself that the Holy Spirit brought to light for me to see after his death. Through much prayer, fasting, wise counsel, worship, studying of the Word, and sound teaching, I was able to deal with my issues. My issues had to be dealt with aside from Jeff because they were mine. Most, if not all, of my issues were there before Jeff came into the picture, and they were there when he left. Sometimes, many times, God has to break us all the way down to get us to where we are supposed to be. This breakdown usually involves a stripping and cutting away of things and even people whom we hold near and dear to our hearts. Sometimes, as was the case with me, it takes a total separation from those people and things for you to really live life the way God intended you to live it—in freedom! My mom used to say something that she heard one of her teachers in the Gospel say—"God will either make you holy in your marriage or coming out of it, but either way you're going to be holy!"

In no way have I "arrived" or gotten to the place where I want to be yet, but I know I am much better out of my marriage than I was while I was in it. This is only because I took the time to allow God to work on *me*. This work should have been done a long time ago, but I thank God for grace, so it's better late than never. Jeff's death was definitely a low place for me, but it was a necessary place for me to be because it evoked desperation within me. I knew if God did not help me, heal me, hear me, provide for me, keep my mind, and the list goes on, I would not make it. So, I allowed Him to do what needed to be done in my life and in me during my grieving process despite my discomfort and uncertainty.

Through this process of facing who I was and what my issues were, I learned to trust and depend totally on God. Losing my husband, house, independence, and consistent provision as I knew it, gave me no other choice but also reminded me of some things. It reminded me God was really my source. I was reminded of how He will never leave nor forsake me. I was reminded of how jealous He was and is for me. Although I had never turned from God, I had other idols before Him, not realizing it mattered to Him so greatly. I had put those things before God and was out of order. So, as I faced myself, I also had to repent. I had to turn and change my mind about how I had been thinking and living. I had to truly start seeing God as THE source and THE provider, not man, not my husband, not my job, and not the military. I am so grateful I can say He has been just that for me throughout these last few years. He has never forsaken us and has always provided!

Facing yourself and seeing the real you are necessary if you are going to heal properly and fully. To become whole, you must first get all of the fragmented pieces out. Those fragments will be ugly, sharp, out of position, out of alignment, and all over the place, but they must be identified and removed before any repairs can be done. Yes, taking out those fragmented pieces will cause you some hurt and pain, but the temporary pain from taking them out is not nearly as bad as the permanent damage that comes from leaving them in. Embrace the grieving process as a time to be emptied out and broken down so you can ultimately be put back together again.

Guilty, Not Guilty

It can be difficult, if not impossible, to identify and address the guilt of your children if you yourself feel any sense of guilt. Guilt can be a slick little bugger in that it can have you feeling like it is a justifiable feeling. Guilt during a period of grief can creep in and really make it seem as though it is natural and just the way it is when these kinds of situations happen. I beg to differ though. Guilt is not something anyone is meant to carry or live with. While it is a very feeling, that does not mean it is valid or it belongs to the individual. I had to recognize and grab ahold of this for myself after Jeff's death.

Almost immediately, I took on some thoughts and feelings of guilt. Was I not a good wife to him? Did I not pray enough? How could he die like that and me not know something was wrong? Did I miss the signs? These are just some of the thoughts that helped to pad the guilt I felt initially. I remember having someone ask me how I was handling the fact that he committed suicide while we were married. Basically, they wanted to know how my "guilt level" was. This comment bothered me at the time, but I realized what this person said was probably what many people who knew my situation thought about as well. Thankfully, at the time when this was presented to me, I was out of that place of guilt I had initially felt. I was able to say what he did was his choice and I carried no guilt about it. The bottom line is when a person takes their own life, those who are left are not at fault and should not be faulted.

There are definitely times when people may contribute to a person's depression or negative feelings about themselves, thus, provoking them to harm themselves. However, that was not the case in this situation. It is important to understand suicide is not about those who are "left behind." Suicide is about the person who dies from it. While I initially viewed Jeff's suicide as a selfish act, I realized me holding myself guilty for that action was actually quite selfish. Holding yourself responsible for another person's death when it was self-inflicted means you take the responsibility away from them. When you think about it that way, it really does not make sense. There may have been things you could have done to help had you seen signs…maybe, but then again maybe not. It is not that cut and dry. Ultimately though, the final decision, in the case of suicide, was in their hands, not yours.

I now have plenty of my own decisions to make and be concerned about; I cannot afford to stay in a place of wondering if it was my fault. I do not and will not hold myself accountable for Jeff's decision because it was just that, his. This is not coming from a place of anger, but a place of freedom and truth. By having this mentality, I am able to live free…free from the guilt, stress, pressure, and darkness that tries to come when dealing with suicidal death. Guilt is too heavy a load to carry…so put it down and live!

"Come to Me, all you who labor and are heavy laden, and I will give you rest. Take My yoke upon you and learn from Me, for I am gentle and lowly in heart, and you will find rest for your souls. For My yoke is easy and My burden is light" (Matthew 11:28-30).

A Woman's Fear: Fatherless Children

Less than three months after Jeff's death, I gave birth to our third child, Jasmine. After giving birth, mothers are open, vulnerable, and often very emotional. This was me. Not only had I just experienced the miracle of birth for the third time, but also I had experienced it after coming through the greatest trauma of my life. I was so overwhelmed by the fact that this baby had gone through this traumatic experience with me and still made it out in perfect condition. I knew this birth story could have been different, but here she was, born a day before her due date and a day after my birthday with no complications, just a healthy and beautiful little girl and another one of God's gifts to me.

I felt special, privileged, honored that He trusted me with her life because I knew I was an emotional wreck. Even though I didn't openly display the wreckage, inside, it was there. There were many times I would look at my new baby girl and just begin to weep. Gripped with the thought of her not having or knowing her father, I was overwhelmed with grief for her. How was I supposed to handle and care for this gift that was given to me? It seemed to be too much at times. It didn't make sense to me. Why was she given to me? What would I say to her? How would I explain the fact that her father took his own life just a few months before she was born? How would she feel knowing her siblings got a chance to know and spend time with him but not her? Would she grow up empty and broken? Would she be jealous, angry, bitter, and resentful? Would she be okay?

These were the thoughts and questions that circled around in my mind during the quiet moments I spent holding her and rocking her to sleep. My main concern was whether she would be okay. This was my concern for all of my children but especially her because she would never know him. Over time, I found peace in knowing God is the ultimate Father. He is a father to the fatherless. I know this is something people say all the time, but it takes on real meaning when you need Him to be a father. I had to and still have to pull on this truth as a reminder that yes, my children will be okay because they have a Father who will never leave them. From the youngest to the oldest, they will not have voids in their lives because of a lack of an earthly or biological father because their heavenly Father fills every void! I had to pull on Father God, Abba, for the lives of my children.

I didn't understand it then, but as I went through my process, I learned Abba can do and be what no earthly father can do and be. He makes up for every area of mess up. No human being, man or woman, can love the way God loves His children. His love reaches and heals every empty and broken place. I rest in the knowledge of this truth, and I remind myself of it whenever those thoughts try to creep back in. All of my children will be just fine because they were His before they were mine and they were His before they were his. If you find yourself in a situation like mine, having children with no father, remember this truth, "A father of the fatherless, a defender of widows, Is God in His holy habitation" (Psalms 68:5). It may seem like this is easier said than done but getting through the grieving process healthily depends on it. Choose to put your trust and hope in the Father of all fathers and watch him work in the lives of you and your children "casting all your care upon Him, for He cares for you" (1 Peter 5:7). Don't allow the stress and pressure that comes with having "fatherless" children consume you. If you do, you are bound to stay in a place or sorrow, bitterness, regret, and fear.

"Be anxious for nothing, but in everything by prayer and supplication, with thanksgiving, let your requests be made known to God; and the peace of God, which surpasses all understanding, will guard your hearts and minds through Christ Jesus" (Philippians 4:6-7).

Shock and Confusion

The shock and confusion that came after Jeff's suicide was a hard place for me to get out of. I truly could not for the life of me understand how he could do something like this. Never in a million years did I see this coming. Was our marriage perfect? No. Were we perfect as individuals? No. But suicide? I just didn't understand. Because he came from a broken home himself, I knew it was his greatest desire for us to stay together as a family no matter what. He expressed to me how he felt about being without his father in the home throughout his adolescence. That was something he absolutely did not want for his children, especially his son because it was such a tough experience for him. These were conversations we had. This was what was in his heart. He loved his children. He took pride in being a present father for his son and daughter. So, for him to break up our family and leave his kids fatherless, it just baffled me. I still to this day am surprised at his decision because of how strongly he felt about being around for his kids.

It just didn't make sense to me. If anyone were to ask him, he would say life was good. He would probably say he was "living the dream." You see, Jeff was kind of a big deal in the eyes of many. He was only in the Navy for about seven years but had accomplished so much during that time. As a matter of fact, he had just made chief the year prior, and a couple of months prior to his death he was selected as an officer. Considering his age and the amount of time he was in the service, this was uncommon. He was on top of the world.

People loved him, flocked to him, looked up to him. He pretty much did what he wanted at work, came and went as he pleased. He enjoyed what he did… Ironically, he was a weapons specialist. He was always a hard worker, ever since I can remember. He took pride in what he did. He took pride in knowing he was able to financially provide for his family. He lived life as if he were untouchable—invincible. So, his choice to leave his "dream life" seemed like a very strange and drastic choice. When people ask me, if I saw signs or had any idea that he would do this, my answer is always "No, never in a million years." To the naked eye, his decision just did not add up.

Anger

I was angry—period, point blank. How could he do this? How could he be so selfish to just end his life and ruin our lives at the same time? These were the thoughts that went through my head early on during my process of grieving. I was angry with him for being inconsiderate of our family. I was angry with him because I was carrying a child in my womb who would never know her father. I was angry with him because I was now the single parent I never wanted to be. I was angry with him for putting me in this position, a position I didn't sign up for. Now, I would have to be the one to clean up the mess he made. I would be the one to have to try to explain to our children his reason for doing what he did. How was I supposed to teach our son how to be a man? Who would teach him how to treat a lady? Who would teach him how to submit to authority? Who would teach him how to dress and present himself as a young black boy and man? How was I supposed to fill those shoes? Who would talk to his son about how to deal with police and police brutality?

My son would no longer have a father to teach him the things fathers are supposed to teach their sons, and this angered me greatly because I felt like it wasn't supposed to be this way. It didn't have to be this way. How did it end up this way? How was I supposed to give my daughters the attention and affirmation they would need? How would they know they are truly beautiful and a gift to be treasured? Who would tell them they are pretty and get them to really believe it? How would they know what to look for in a husband? How would they know men could be trusted? How would they know a father's love is a good kind of love? How would all of my children view God because of their father's absence?

I was upset. He literally made a life-altering decision, but it didn't just alter his life. It altered the lives of our children. I was not even angry because of him leaving me because, that, I could deal with. It was the fact that he left our children, in their innocence and helplessness, and that angered me deeply. They would not be able to deal with this as easily as I would. Now, I was stuck here to answer the questions and deal with the comments from people who would have something to say. I didn't like it one bit. I was angry because it didn't seem fair.

I was angry, cold, maybe even growing bitter toward the thought and memory of him. Anger is a very real and normal emotion to experience when dealing with death and suicide specifically. In many ways, suicide can feel like a form of betrayal. In my case, I had no clue, not even an inkling of a clue, that he would have killed himself. I was completely blindsided by his death. As I went through my angry period of grief, it honestly felt like I had been betrayed. It was like he kept a secret from me that ultimately destroyed our family. I felt like he copped out, like he bowed out disgracefully. I felt like because stuff got a little challenging he just gave up. He chose not to play life fair, and I got the short end of the stick because of it.

While these were my thoughts and feelings, as real as they were to me at the time, they weren't necessarily right or true. Anger has a tendency to blind a person. The kind of anger I was experiencing, while some of it was warranted, much of it was selfish and prideful because it revolved around how *I* felt and what I felt he did to *me*. I had my time to be angry, but as I mentioned before, it was not him that I needed to focus on, but me.

12

Take Care of YOU

If you've ever flown on an airplane, you've probably heard the flight attendants, during the safety instruction segment, say to secure your own air mask before assisting others, including your children. While this always seemed strange to me, going through my grief process, I finally understood why it is actually sensible. As mothers, it is instinctive for us to want to help our children first when dangerous situations arise. Think about it. For example, we have our children walk on the "inside" when walking on the curb outside next to the street so they are less vulnerable to cars, leaving us vulnerable instead. Our mindset is a good one in that we want to keep our children out of harm's way and as safe as possible. We want them to be alive and well to live full and healthy lives.

We often neglect our own health and livelihood for the sake of our children. We run around all over the place making sure the children have what they need and get where they need to go. This is part of the role of a mother. However, it is not within the role of a mother to run herself ragged in the process. The reason we are instructed to secure our own mask first is because if we help our children first, we will be no good if we are then unable to breathe ourselves. Who can we assist then? Who will be there for the children then? I truly believe this concept needs to be carried over into everyday life, and in this case, the lives of grieving mothers. If you as the mother are not well, healthy and whole, there is no way you can effectively take care of your children. Their health—physical, mental, and spiritual—and life's prosperity is in many ways dependent upon yours.

Right after Jeff died and for a while after, I would experience feelings of guilt as it pertained to my own self-care. I would feel bad about wanting to get my hair or nails done. I would feel bad about wanting to buy something for myself or going out with friends. I felt like I needed to be with my children all of the time and like I shouldn't be spending money on anyone except them. While there is some truth to this, the problem with these feelings and this mentality is that there is no balance. Should you always go hang out? No! Should you always and only spend money on yourself? Absolutely not! But to completely cut yourself off from doing the things you enjoy and the things that make you happy is unrealistic and just not right. Neglecting your own personal needs and occasional wants is not the answer to creating an environment conducive to healing. As a grieving woman, give yourself permission to be happy. Get your hair and nails done. Go shopping and order from your favorite restaurant. Even beyond the outward pleasures, take care or your inner-self as well. Keep up with your physical health; make time to exercise. Also, make sure just as you book appointments for your children to visit the doctor and dentist, you do the same for yourself. The grieving process is not the time to let yourself go.

Although it may be easy to fall into that place of not caring and not paying attention to what you look like or how you feel, you cannot afford to stay in that place. Make a conscious effort to do the opposite of what you may be feeling. On those days, and there will be many, when you feel like crap on the inside, shower and comb your hair at the very least. If you can muster up enough strength, put on an outfit that looks and feels good on you. These simple actions can do wonders for shifting your mood. Not only that, but it shows your children you are still present and in the moment with them. They will be able to see you are still the mother they knew before the death. Although there will be some changes, they will have a sense of familiarity and peace in seeing you put together. Again, there must be a balance to this because there will be some days when you just cannot or do not want to look your best or be "put together." There will be days when you don't want to get out of the bed, and you couldn't care less about a shower or the hair that is standing up all over your head. That happens, and it is normal.

As a part of taking care of you during the grief process, I suggest getting yourself a therapist. I mentioned this in regard to children earlier on in this book, but I believe having one for yourself is equally important. I remember going into my first session unsure of what it would be like. I made up in my mind beforehand what I would and would not share. I told myself I was okay and over the whole situation regarding Jeff's death. I convinced myself I was just going for the kids, but I did not really need it for myself because I was all good. I was so used to being private with my business that going to a therapist just seemed weird, and I really was not sure what if anything I'd get out of it. But I was willing to go because I figured it couldn't hurt. Not only that, but I also knew that it would be important for my children to see me taking some of the same steps toward healing as them. They would be able to see that just as they have to deal with their feelings and emotions surrounding their father's death, so would I.

The first couple of sessions I remember my jaws being so tight as I told my story. I was tense, and I was angry, though I thought I was okay. I held back my tears because I told myself I was done crying and did not want to cry anymore. I was so used to being strong and holding it all together I was determined to sit up straight in that office and act as though I was unbothered. Eventually, I broke, and my eyes and heart began to open from my time spent in that therapist's office. Levels of healing took place in that room for me as I let the truth speak in a non-judgmental, no pressure environment. I would go home each time with assignments that would help push me toward healing, wholeness, and freedom.

Self-care is important because without it, as a grieving mother, you are more prone to literally losing your mind or dying from a faint heart. This death may not be physical, but it's still an unnatural death that affects your children. If you "die" there is no way you can truly be available to care for your children. We must not get so caught up and wrapped up in our children that we suffer in the process. One of the best things we can do for them is be healthy and whole. Children often follow and model the pattern set for them by their parents. Let your children see you thrive through adversity. Let them see you dress up. Let them see you put effort into making each day a day of purpose and meaning. Let them see you caring for yourself and loving yourself. Let them see you ask for help when you need it. Let them see you are an imperfect human being with feelings and needs. Let them see balance throughout your process even as you learn or relearn how to take care of you.

There is a time and place for everything. Grief has a time, and for some, the grieving process can take a long time. Therefore, it is hard to put a time limit on it. However, throughout the process of grief, there will be ups and downs…good days and not so good days. In these moments, life still must go on, but intentionality must kick in. If you are not intentional about life going on, it can be easy to fall into a state of depression. Being intentional about life may look like planning activities, exercising, enrolling in school, and making yourself spend time with friends and family even when you don't want to.

A Time to Mourn

Healing properly after the grieving process has a lot to do with maturity. This is specifically the case for adults who are going through the process of grief. The choice to become bitter or better is something to consider. As a woman whose husband committed suicide while I was pregnant with our third child, I had every reason to become bitter. I chose instead to become better from my experience. I made the choice to become a better mother, sister, daughter, and friend. Ultimately, I made the choice to become a better woman overall by journeying through the process of dealing with the areas of myself that needed attention.

So, what happens when the time for grieving is over? Do you face the music realizing your loved one is never coming back? Or do you continue to hold on to false hope and a dream of what was, could have been, or might still be? To heal properly, it is necessary to deal with what your reality is. My reality was my husband was dead. My reality was I would now be a single mother of three young children, maybe just for a season, but possibly forever. My reality was I would have to uproot my family and move back home. My reality was I would have to do things I never wanted to do. My reality was I would have to do things I should not have to do. My reality was my life and the lives of my children would not seem fair. My reality was my life would turn out much differently than I had planned. My reality was not everyone, hardly anyone probably, would understand my reality.

Ecclesiastes 3:1-8 tells us:

1 "To everything, there is a season and a time to every purpose under the heaven:
2 A time to be born, and a time to die; a time to plant, and a time to pluck up that which is planted;
3 A time to kill, and a time to heal; a time to break down, and a time to build up;
4 A time to weep, and a time to laugh; a time to mourn, and a time to dance;
5 A time to cast away stones, and a time to gather stones together; a time to embrace, and a time to refrain from embracing;
6 A time to get, and a time to lose; a time to keep, and a time to cast away;
7 A time to rend, and a time to sew; a time to keep silence, and a time to speak;
8 A time to love, and a time to hate; a time of war, and a time of peace."

A big part of taking care of yourself is allowing yourself to mourn for a season (what this season looks like will vary), but then also ensuring you don't stay in mourning forever. I could stay in a place of "woe is me" or I could choose to just deal with it because "it" was now my life. I am a firm believer of what my good friend and sister Reese told me shortly after Jeff died. She basically said children heal based on how their parent heals. I believe me choosing to grow, learn, and thrive through this process has much to do with why my children are doing so as well. They have been given automatic rights and permission to blossom and be happy because their mother is doing just that. They have been given permission to take the time to grieve and sort out their thoughts, feelings, and emotions because I did the same thing.

This issue of healing, or moving on as I like to call it, after grieving is not a matter of being insensitive or harsh. It is a matter of life or death. Choosing to be better is choosing life while choosing to be bitter is choosing death.

God and Me
Walking with God is what kept me healthy throughout my process of grief. Had I not had a relationship with Him, I would not be the person I

am today nor would I be where I am today. I would have, without a doubt, lost my mind. You see, death of any kind is not for the faint of heart. Death by suicide, though, is in a category all its own. This is not to boast about myself at all, but rather to boast about the Goodness and Faithfulness of God. From the very moment I stepped into that cold and bloody bathroom, He had me. I knew He was with me. I felt Him; I spoke to Him; He spoke to me; I heard Him—He was there. I knew I would be okay and life was going to be just fine although I did not know exactly how.

As soon as I walked into the bathroom and saw his body in that tub, I knew a shift had just taken place…the shift from death to life for both he and I. His life had just ended, but I knew mine was just beginning. I would have to learn how to live again, and God would be my teacher. My mother was on to something when she named me since one of the meanings for Moriah is "God is my teacher." I should have bugged out right then and there in that bathroom, but instead, I was calm. I was able to pull myself together and handle my business as if everything was okay in those moments at the scene of Jeff's death.

I can remember walking through Target in Honolulu with my then two children just days after his death. I was pushing a shopping cart and literally felt like I was floating. It was like an out-of-body experience. It was as if I was not even there although I obviously was there and visible. I called my mom on the phone at that time and told her what I was experiencing because it freaked me out. I had no strength in my body. I wanted to just drop to the floor and lay there because I was so overwhelmed by everything that was going on and everything that needed to be done whenever a spouse dies—planning the funeral, making sure all of his affairs are in order, and so much more. It felt as though I was moving, but not using my own strength to do it.

I truly believe the angels of the Lord were there carrying me…gently assisting me so I could get done what needed to be done. This is just one example out of many times I physically felt God's presence with me during my process. He was gentle with me in the beginning because I needed Him to be. He showed Himself as Comforter because that's who I needed Him to be at that time. I was fragile, open, sensitive, broken, and afraid in the early stages of my grief. So, He met me where I was and held me and loved me and ministered to me from those places.

It's Bigger than You

I used to think talking about Jeff to the kids would only make things worse. I believed bringing up memories of him would cause more damage to them than good. I thought they would be reduced to tears at the mention of his name. This is what I thought. I later realized and had to come to terms with the idea and possible fact that perhaps I was the one who would be the most agitated by this. The truth of the matter was I had gotten over his death, but my children were in a different place than I was. I was okay with not talking about him. I was okay with not mentioning his birthday when it was that time of year. I no longer had thoughts of him as I did in the beginning. I was living life, and I was just fine going along without him or the memory of him as it related to our relationship together.

This was all from the perspective of me the "woman and wife" and not me the "mother." What I had to remind myself was that although his status of being my husband had changed, his status of being the father of my children had not. I really had to take a step back and see and feel from the perspective of my children. It is very likely they will always miss their father. It is also very likely they may not ever mention this to me for whatever reason. Them not mentioning it does not mean it is not an issue or an important factor that needs to be addressed. As their mother and the person responsible for their wellbeing, it is my job to mention it. I had to get over myself for the sake of my children because their process is and will continue to be different from mine. While I have already been detached from him, they will forever have an attachment and connection to him.

It took me some time to get to the place where I was ready and willing to celebrate their father. Many factors played into my initial reluctance. I was afraid talking about their father would bring up feelings of sorrow and pain for my children, so I avoided it for the most part. From time to time I would do what I called check-ins with them. I would go to them separately, usually at bedtime or during our outings, and ask them about how they were doing. I would ask them if they wanted to talk about anything or ask me anything. I would ask them how they were doing in regard to their father's death. Not much would come from these check-ins, but I felt like I was at least trying in that area.

For a while, I made little effort at talking about their father mainly because I just did not want to. Part of me was still annoyed because he took his own life and left his children in this predicament. Other reasons included that I really just wanted to move on. I felt that if I mentioned him to the children or shared memories, it would somehow mean I was still attached to him and thinking about him. While I was not thinking about him for myself personally, I knew my children probably thought about him quite often. This way of thinking and being was totally selfish of me, but it was where I was at that time. I knew I was really healing and going in the right direction when I was able to celebrate and talk about him with my children openly and freely.

I saw this change in myself on Veterans Day 2017. This would be the first time I really celebrated Jeff since his death. My children's school was having a Veterans Day program that parents were invited to. I asked Trinity specifically if she wanted me to come. She made it very clear she wanted me there. After all she had been going through emotionally with missing her dad, I knew I needed to be there and wanted to be there to support her. I wasn't sure how she would react during the program, hearing the stories of those who may have held the same position as her father in the U.S. Navy.

I sat there on that Friday morning, unsure of what the program would entail but proud of myself for even just showing up. Soon, the guest speaker was introduced. To my surprise, he was indeed, someone who held a similar position to Jeff. He was a retired Naval Officer who happened to be on submarines just like Jeff. As I sat there next to her during the assembly in the school chapel on that Friday, I found myself looking over at her to check her facial expression at different times. I wanted to make sure she was okay and the content was not too much for her. To my surprise, both she and her brother, who was sitting a couple rows behind me with friends, were engaged and had looks of interest and excitement on their faces. The speaker shared a ton of cool facts about the military, and he highlighted the Navy more than anything of course.

As he shared facts about submarines, I leaned over and told Trinity her father used to do the same kinds of things the speaker was describing. Her eyes lit up as she said, "He did?!" I was proud to tell her about the kind of guy her dad was in the military. I was happy to see her receive all of this information so well. I knew both Jeffrey and Trinity felt proud of their father in that chapel that day. They probably stuck their chests out a little, with their chins up, and thought about the fact that their dad was an important man who helped our country. It made my heart smile to see them in this environment, on this occasion, doing so well.

Upon leaving the school that morning after the program, I had a strong urge to continue in this mode of celebration and memorial. I knew I needed to take the time to sit down with my children and give them space, or rather create a space for them to share memories of their father, not just in reference to him being in the military and it being Veterans Day, but in a general sense. My acknowledgment of him on that day at their school opened the door for another level of healing for all of us, and I was determined to keep the momentum going.

I decided I would let Trinity in on this by asking her if she wanted to do something to celebrate Veterans Day later that evening. I knew by me presenting this to her, I would be held accountable for my word because children never forget when you tell them you'll do something! So, I intentionally had this conversation with her just in case I had thoughts of pulling out at the last minute. That evening, I took my three children to one of their father's favorite restaurants for an early dinner after school.

As we sat down at the table, I laid down the ground rules for the night. No phones…no playing games on my phone (for them), and no texting or social media (for me). I explained to them our reason for being at the restaurant was to celebrate and remember their father for Veterans Day. I let them know we would be sharing memories of him and they could ask me any questions they had about him. I had them take turns sharing memories.

I watched as their faces lit up as they remembered. They remembered how fun he was. They remembered going outside and playing football with him. They remembered him and still saw him as "super dad," and I was glad. I was thankful they were so open about him this night. I was thankful they still respected and cherished him despite the circumstances surrounding his death. There were a couple of memories shared that Trinity could not remember, but I was able to chime in and help refresh her memory. I reminded them both of some of the fun and silly times they had with him.

We all smiled and laughed at dinner that night as we shared stories and memories and it felt good. I knew I was healing and moving forward and my children were too. I was not angry, sad, or bitter. I acknowledged that he deserved to be celebrated on Veterans Day but more importantly, in the lives of my children simply because he was their father. The fact that he committed suicide did not matter at this point.

What mattered was my children were still alive and well and because of that, remembering him in this way was necessary for their continued growth and healing. It was necessary for all of us. That night at dinner I asked my children an important question that may seem obvious to some. I asked them why it was important to share memories of their father. We decided doing so would help them not to forget him and would be helpful for their baby sister. I reminded them Jasmine would never know him, so they would be the ones who would be able to tell her all about him. I reminded them of how they had the opportunity to know him and spend time with him, not to create a sense of guilt in them but rather gratefulness. We talked about talking about him more often.

I let them know I was always open to talk and share memories when they wanted to. They both agreed going out to dinner and sharing in the way we did was helpful for them. I had come a long way from not being able or willing to say his name aloud because of anger and ill feelings, to actually having an entire intentional and positive conversation about him and for that, I am grateful.

13

Moving on After Good Grief

After reading this book, you may be asking yourself, what is good grief exactly? In a nutshell, "good grief" is grief that leads you in the direction of healing and wholeness. With that being said, I believe grieving is necessary and there is a right way to do it. Grief should be looked at as something that takes time…a process. Good grief involves the acknowledgment of the death of something or someone. This means you cannot grieve the right way if you are in denial or unwilling to accept the truth. At the same time, grieving right does not mean that the loved one has to be forgotten. Good grief does not guarantee the absence of sorrow and pain, but on the contrary, there will most likely be evidence of some of that at some point during the process. Good grief involves forward movement. If you remain stuck in the past, chances are you are not experiencing good grief. When you grieve the right way, you are able to move from bitter to better, and you embrace the future.

Good grief is not a cookie cutter process. What it looks like will vary from person to person and it depends on other facts such as age and relational factors. Adults may not grieve the same way children do. Teenagers may not grieve the same way young children will. But the overall point to grieving properly is to allow yourself to even grieve at all and then getting the support needed to go through the process with the goal of overcoming your grief. I believe grief must be overcome because it is not something meant to last forever. Overcoming grief does not mean the loved one is not loved or missed, it simply gives you the permission to move on or move forward with life without feeling bad about doing so. Good grief says, "Grieve, but don't stop living!"

Life is meant to be lived out on this earth. Living out this life comes with the very real likelihood that we will need to deal with many trials and heartaches, including death. However, none of these things are meant to keep us in a place of sorrow, fear, and stagnation. "The thief does not come except to steal, and to kill, and to destroy. I have come that they may have life, and that they may have it more abundantly" (John 10:10). We can get through them and come out on the other side intact, stronger than before, and full of joy (yes joy) if we make a choice and put forth the effort to do so.

Moving Forward

"To console those who mourn in Zion, to give them beauty for ashes, The oil of joy for mourning, the garment of praise for the spirit of heaviness; That they may be called trees of righteousness, the planting of the Lord, that He may be glorified" (Isaiah 61:3).

I would have never thought I would be starting life over. I would have never thought the thought of suicide would hit so close to home. I would have never thought my children would be without their father. Three years ago, I never would have imagined my life turning out the way it did. Having said all of that, I must say I have no regrets. What I have learned, experienced, and seen during my process has helped me to grow and get to the place I am in now. I am in a much better place because I am a much better me. My grief process has taught me so much about myself, my children, and my God and I can't say I would trade those lessons. While I never wanted tragedy to hit my family, I am grateful it was used for good. I truly believe not one trial or experience we go through in life is wasted. I chose to find the purpose in the pain of all that I experienced. I chose to live and not die because it is a choice. I chose to continue this journey to life while supporting and encouraging my children to do so as well.

It is with great joy and relief I can say I have and still am moving forward. Whenever someone hears my testimony of becoming a widow after losing my husband to suicide, the look on their face and their entire demeanor completely changes. They are usually shocked and saddened, some to the point of tears. I have found myself throughout my grief journey having to console others and assure them that I really am okay. They are then left with a look of amazement and wonder as to how I could possibly be doing okay.

My wellness is a testament to grieving the right way. It is a testament to what it looks like and how important it is to stand on your faith in the midst of a time when everything, including your faith seems to have been shaken. Good grief involves a testing and proving of your faith. For me, my faith was in God. My faith was in trusting that He would bring us through with little to no damage.

As you consider pursuing your own journey to life after dealing with death, please also consider the fact that moving forward for you may look completely different than it does for someone else. We must be careful that we don't allow the opinions and reactions of others to get in the way of our journey and our process. As you move forward, you may have to do things that others don't. You may have to change parts of you or your life that others don't understand or agree with. This journey is a journey that only *you* can take. Your process is a process that is designed for *you* to go through. While you may be fortunate enough to have people that can walk with you at some points as support, much of this will be you going it alone because ultimately it is *your* life that is at stake.

For the people that witnessed you go through your process, your decision to move on may seem strange to them. For others, they may expect you to "move on" sooner than you may be ready for. You must guard yourself against this as well. Those who love and care about you may be eager to see you move on with life according to what their definition of moving on means. I was often questioned about whether or not I was dating or had a desire to remarry throughout my journey, even early on. Don't be moved or become frustrated by what family or those who are familiar with your situation may say. You don't owe an explanation as to why your process looks the way it does. Move on at your own pace and based on what that means for you.

There were specific steps and decisions I had to make along my journey in order for me to make forward movement. One of the biggest and perhaps most impactful decisions was to go back to my maiden name. This was not an easy choice for many reasons but it was one that I personally knew I needed to make. To outsiders looking in, and even to some family, it may not make sense. It may even appear that it was too drastic of a decision. I knew that for me it was necessary because it symbolized establishment and identity.

I mentioned earlier, that I never really knew who I was a part from my late husband. Going back to my father's name has helped me express outwardly where my journey has brought me to inwardly. No fingers pointed, no blame, no grudges or regrets. My grief process and journey brought me back to *me* and helped me to establish who I was then, who I am now, and even who I will be in the future. This was huge for me!

I had to come to the realization that life was going to go on with or without me, but either way, life was going to happen! I can now say I look forward to the future. I have vision for my family's future and present. No longer do I look back at my past and all I've lost. No longer do I have pity parties. No longer do I have the "woe is me" feelings. I know good grief will continue to be a process for my children and is just getting started for my youngest. As she has just recently began asking about her father almost every day now. I know her grief process will probably look completely different from her siblings, but I am ready for it, and I know she will be just fine. I will continue to ask for more grace as I journey alongside my kids as they progress.

In the meantime, I can honestly say I have joy and peace. Life is good for us. As a matter of fact, I am living the best life I have ever lived so far. I know that many have been and still are skeptical as to whether or not I am doing as well as I say I am. I can assure you that this joy and peace I have is real and cannot be taken away from me because I have made the choice to keep it!

So whether you or your children are grieving the loss of a spouse, a parent, or a loved one, you have the choice to claim joy and peace as your own as well. You have the ability to grieve and to grieve right. Doing this, will allow you the freedom to move forward and make it through the journey to life after death.

> **You have turned for me my mourning into dancing; You have put off my sackcloth and clothed me with gladness, to the end that my glory may sing praise to You and not be silent. O Lord my God, I will give thanks to You forever.**
>
> **Psalm 30:11**

Acknowledgments

Thank You, God, my Father, my Savior, my Keeper, for arming me with the strength to go through all that I have gone through. Thank You for loving me unconditionally. Thank You for never leaving my side and remaining Consistent in my life. Without You I would not have made it. You are my Everything and I love You with all that is within me!

To my children, Jeffrey, Trinity, and Jasmine, thank you for loving me and for teaching me what strength and resilience look like. You are the bravest, most courageous children I know! I am so grateful to have been chosen as your mom. Keep healing, growing, inspiring, and teaching others! Shine your light!

Mom, thank you for your support and wise counsel through the darkest of times in my life. Thank you for always interceding. Your prayers, no doubt, made a difference in the outcome of my life. I love and appreciate you more than words can express. It has been such a privilege and an honor to be able to watch you and learn from you. Thank you for leading by example.

Dad, thank you for your wisdom, strength, and presence. Thank you for coming to see about me at a time when I needed you the most. That will forever be a memory etched in my heart that contributed to my healing. Mom Alicia, thank you for your prayers, encouragement, and constant reminders of what the Word says.

To my Godparents, Greg and Joan, thank you for your consistency, wisdom, and love throughout this journey. Thank you for stepping up and giving extra love, support, and attention to my children even though you didn't have to. We are blessed to have you in our lives.

To Jeannine, we've been through the good, the bad, and the ugly together! Thank you for taking a chance on me. Thank you for being patient. Your presence, advice, and encouragement as a sister, a friend, and a woman have been nothing other than a gift from God. Thank you for speaking life over me when I wasn't able to!

To Apostle Joshua Giles and my Kingdom Embassy family, thank you for welcoming us with open arms at a time when we were so fragile. The sound teaching, atmosphere of praise and worship, and the love that was shown, helped to push us through to where we are now.

To my "village", thank you for being positive influences in the lives of my children throughout their journey thus far. Thank you for your support and your time. Thank you for looking out for them and speaking life over them. Thank you for hugging them and loving on them. Thank you for simply being there and making yourself available. I appreciate you all. Nothing you have done has gone unnoticed.

To all of our family near and far, thank you for all of your love, support, and encouragement.

To everyone that stepped in and helped during our time of immediate need in Hawaii, thank you so much. Thank you for going above and beyond for us. Your selfless actions will never be forgotten.

To everyone who supported us in some way, thank you. We appreciate you all. May God bless you!

About the Author

Moriah Friend is a mother, educator, writer, and leader who has worked in the field of early childhood education for several years. With the heart to help nurture and educate children, she received a Bachelor of Arts in Early Childhood Education Administration and a Master of Education. Furthermore, it has been her desire to see hurting women and children become restored and whole so that they can live their best life. Her greatest joy has come from raising and nurturing her three children ages 11, 8, and 3 years old. Moriah currently resides in Minneapolis, MN with her family.